GREAT SCIENTISTS

AMERICAN PROFILES

GREAT SCIENTISTS

■

Victoria Sherrow

Facts On File, Inc.

For Walter Newton

———

Great Scientists

Facts On File, Inc.
11 Penn Plaza
New York NY 10001

Library of Congress Cataloging-in-Publication Data
Sherrow, Victoria.
  Great scientists / Victoria Sherrow
    p. cm.—(American profiles)
  Includes bibliographical references and index.
  Summary: Profiles eight American scientists who have made important contributions to twentieth-century science, including Thomas Hunt Morgan, Robert Oppenheimer, and Linus Pauling.
  ISBN 0-8160-2540-1
  1. Scientists—United States—Biography—Juvenile literature.
  2. Science—History—20th century—Juvenile literature.
  [1. Scientists.] I. Title. II. Series: American profiles (Facts On File, Inc.)
  Q141.S465   1992
  509'.2'2—dc20
  [B]   91-33848

Facts On File books are available at special discounts when purchased in bulk quantities for businesses, associations, institutions, or sales promotions. Please call our Special Sales Department in New York at 212/967-8800 or 800/322-8755.

You can find Facts On File on the World Wide Web at http://www.factsonfile.com

Text and cover design by Ron Monteleone

Printed in the United States of America

MP FOF 10 9 8 7 6 5 4 3

This book is printed on acid-free paper.

Contents

Introduction

*T*he 20th century has been a time of breakthroughs in every field of science. The atom, once thought to be the smallest particle of matter, has been split. Atomic energy has been harnessed for wartime and peacetime uses. The minute world of the living cell has been explored, revealing secrets of heredity, growth, and disease. Scientists have not only solved many of the mysteries of life and matter on Earth, they have developed methods by which people can learn about—and even travel to—outer space.

As the century began, knowledge about matter was expanding in amazing ways. Science had already made great strides since ancient times when Greek thinkers concluded that everything in the world was made of four elements—earth, fire, air, and water. By the 1900s, scientists knew that matter was much more complex, although they had yet to probe the structure of the atom itself.

One crucial discovery came in 1895, when a German scientist, Wilhelm Röntgen, discovered X rays in his laboratory. Röntgen found that some mysterious, invisible rays could penetrate cardboard and even a door, causing chemicals to glow with light. Then, in 1896, Frenchman Henri Becquerel detected the radioactivity that occurs naturally in uranium. One year later, British physicist J. J. Thomson showed that the rays described by Röntgen and Becquerel were made up of minute, subatomic particles that moved at incredibly fast speeds. These particles were named *electrons*. Scientists began to understand that atoms have minute, functioning parts.

In the early 1900s, the study of radioactive substances led to medical advances (for example, the use of X rays to look through living tissue). Scientists from various countries studied the composition and behavior of the atom, often by studying cosmic rays. These sources of radiation arise naturally, seemingly from outer space, and reach the Earth by penetrating the atmosphere. Some cosmic rays hold as much energy as billions of electron volts. During the 1930s, American Nobel laureate Arthur H. Compton led a worldwide survey of these baffling radiations.

Years of scientific research culminated in the creation of the first atomic bombs. This newspaper is from the day an atomic bomb was first dropped on Japan.

(Courtesy of Los Alamos National Laboratory)

Introduction

After finding radioactivity in nature, scientists learned to create radioactivity—either by building atoms up or by ripping them apart. Before the 1900s, scientists had thought that matter could not be created or destroyed and that, likewise, energy could not be created or destroyed. These beliefs were radically altered by the idea that mass could be converted into energy. This came about in large part because of Albert Einstein's revolutionary theories of relativity and his famous formula of mass-energy equivalence: $E = mc^2$ (stated simply, energy equals mass multiplied by the velocity of light, squared.) Now, people know that the destruction of matter can unleash vast amounts of energy. After centuries of using heat and light from the sun or from sources that get *their* energy from the sun, it has become possible for people to use energy from the atom. Decades of probing the atom climaxed in 1945 with the explosion of atomic bombs whose power came from the splitting of the atomic nuclei of uranium or plutonium.

As important as the discovery of atomic energy are the amazing 20th century advances in the life sciences. One milestone was the unraveling of the structure of proteins. In 1900, the German chemist Emil Fischer found that protein, which forms the major tissues in all animals, was made up of carbon, nitrogen, hydrogen, oxygen, and other elements, linked in chains of amino acids. The pattern of these chains was unknown until 1951, when U.S. chemist Linus Pauling and his colleagues worked out the structure of protein. In doing so, Pauling had applied his knowledge of physics, biology, and chemistry. This merging of scientific fields has been another trend during the 1900s.

When the century began, biologists were eager to answer two major questions: How does a fertilized egg grow into a fully formed, living adult? And, how do traits pass from one generation to another—in other words, what is the mechanism of inheritance? Information grew as scientists from various countries studied living cells. In America, Thomas Hunt Morgan conducted long-term studies of the inheritance patterns of fruit flies. He played a major role in building the new field of genetics. Later, American James D. Watson and British scientist Francis Crick deciphered the structure of the building block of genes, which carries the "code of inheritance"—the DNA molecule.

After the molecular structure of DNA was understood, scientists worked to figure out how DNA carried and transmitted information. The results of DNA research have been far-reaching. Scientists have figured out how living things grow and reproduce. They have even created DNA in the laboratory. DNA research showed scientists how mutations—changes in genes—occur when sections of DNA are changed either by natural or artificial means. There is a controversial field called genetic engineering, in which genes are cut, spliced, and put into different combinations.

American scientists played a key role in these 20th-century advances, unlike past centuries when Europeans made the major contributions. America's free public education system had improved, in an atmosphere that encouraged individualism and achievement. More well-educated teachers were available and wealth from private and public sources had been used to build and equip universities.

The field of physics is a prime example. During the 1800s and early 1900s, American students often attended European universities to become proficient physicists. By the 1940s, thanks to scientists such as Arthur Compton, Italian-born Enrico Fermi, and J. Robert Oppenheimer, America's physics programs were second to none. There were also excellent programs in biology, chemistry, and other sciences.

Lecturing in America in the winter of 1872–73, British physicist John Tyndall was among those who predicted that science would advance there. He said, "You have scientific genius among you. Take all unnecessary impediments out of its way. Keep your sympathetic eye on the originator of knowledge. Give him the freedom necessary for his researches. . . ."

A number of great American scientists, including several of those in this book, had to overcome impediments, including a lack of money for higher education and slim research funds. Albert Einstein and Enrico Fermi also faced oppressive Fascist governments in their birthplaces, leading them to become U.S. citizens.

Without family money to help them, Linus Pauling, Robert Goddard, Enrico Fermi, and James Watson had to find ways to finance their schooling and research. They worked at jobs, got financial aid, and/or attended inexpensive colleges.

Struggling to build his rockets with begged, borrowed, or junkyard materials, Goddard survived for years on grants from the private Guggenheim Foundation and the public Smithsonian Institution. Thomas Hunt Morgan saved money for genetic experiments by keeping cheap glass milk bottles and bits of used envelopes to house the fruit flies he was studying.

During World War II, the U.S. government supported scientific research in an unprecedented way. Science was seen as critical for the national defense, so the government spent $2 billion to build the first nuclear bombs. As part of that effort, Fermi, who had run his Roman laboratory on a shoestring budget, now had enough equipment and staff to develop the first self-sustaining nuclear chain reaction. And Oppenheimer, scientific director of the project to build the bomb, had the resources to complete this work. In July 1945, Oppenheimer's team at Los Alamos, New Mexico, watched the results when the world's first nuclear bomb exploded over the desert.

To build the bomb, scientists from many nations had worked together. Concern about a common enemy—Nazi Germany— united people from Hungary, Italy, Poland, Denmark, Great Britain, the Soviet Union, Germany, and the United States, among others. Adolf Hitler had curtailed academic freedom in Germany and the other countries that his armies occupied. The Nazis decreed what people could read, hear, discuss, and study. Scientists who protested against Nazism lost their jobs, were persecuted along with Jews, and fled to unoccupied nations, chiefly the United States, where their skills enriched American science. Hitler's policies of oppression and bigotry enabled the Allies to assemble the most talented scientific brainpool in history.

The 1940s saw a historic collaboration of people from different countries working toward common goals. They worked in secret and under tremendous pressure. Before, secrecy had been rare and unpopular among scientists, who were used to publishing and discussing their work openly.

The onset of the atomic age united science and politics. Now that nuclear weapons could destroy life on Earth, nations had to face the chance of being annihilated by faraway enemies. The potential cost of war was suddenly unthinkably high. The political implications of atomic energy have led countries to discuss needed controls. Yet atomic energy offers a boundless supply of power to improve industry and everyday living throughout the world. Atomic research has aided in the diagnosis and treatment of disease, as well as helping to produce stronger food crops. Because oil, gas, and coal will someday run out, nuclear power is a compact alternative. This was demonstrated in 1954 when the U.S. Navy submarine *Nautilus* began a two-year, 60,000-mile trip carrying for fuel a lump of uranium smaller than a baseball. It would have taken about 720,000 gallons of oil to provide the same energy.

The space age and arms race that followed World War II have vastly increased the amount of public money directed toward scientific research. The scientists who built the bomb were painfully aware of what might result from their work. Several hoped that the destructive force of nuclear weapons would convince people that war was futile. Many complex questions are being debated as all fields of science continue to advance. Is it morally right to develop new life forms or radically change forms of life now on Earth? How much control should humankind exert over its physical destiny? Who should make such decisions? More than at any time in history, 20th-century scientists have seen the outcome of their work. Some have become public figures, discussing the role of science in society. Oppenheimer, Compton, and Pauling are among those who have said that citizens play a key role in scientific debate. People who understand scientific issues can influence the decisions made by scientists and politicians, helping to find ways in which scientific progress can be used to enhance the quality of life.

Thomas Hunt Morgan: Untangling the Secrets of Heredity

Head shot of Morgan at a young age, not dated.
(Courtesy of the National Library of Medicine)

*T*he laboratory was crowded with thousands of milk bottles, piled on shelves along the walls. Inside each bottle were one or more tiny black flies. A tall man with a neatly trimmed beard stood at one desk, his head bent over a microscope. But this April day in 1910, Dr. Thomas Morgan saw something remarkable under the lens: The fly that he was examining had *white eyes*. Yet both of its parents had red eyes, the normal eye color for these insects. After breeding generations of flies for a year, Morgan had found one whose eye color differed from that of both parents. Noticing Morgan's excitement, other people in the lab hurried over to see the fly for themselves.

The appearance of the white-eyed male fly in Thomas Hunt Morgan's "fly room" at Columbia University in 1910 was a landmark in the field of heredity—the study of how different traits are passed from parents to their offspring. By breeding this fly with others and analyzing the new flies that were born, Morgan answered questions that had puzzled scientists for centuries. He showed that genes located inside living cells determine eye color and other traits.

The development of the science of genetics by Morgan and others has led to some of the most electrifying discoveries of the 20th century. Genetic research has enabled humans to change the traits of plants and animals. It has provided valuable tools in the fight against many diseases.

Thomas Hunt Morgan was born on September 25, 1866, in Lexington, Kentucky. His father, Charlton Hunt Morgan, was a former Confederate army officer, nephew of the famous general John Hunt Morgan. Charlton Morgan ran a hemp manufacturing business in Lexington and had served as American consul to Sicily, Italy. Thomas's mother, Ellen Key Morgan, was a granddaughter of Francis Scott Key, who wrote what became known as the "Star-Spangled Banner."

Morgan showed an early interest in science. He collected fossils and rocks and examined a variety of birds' eggs before he was 10 years old. A capable student, he began college at age 16, majoring in zoology at the State College of Kentucky (later the University of Kentucky), located in Lexington.

During college, Morgan's interest in animal science continued to grow. He entered graduate school at Johns Hopkins University in Baltimore, Maryland, to study marine biology. There, Morgan majored in morphology (the study of the form and function of organisms) and physiology (the study of the life processes of organisms). He received his Ph.D. in 1890 after writing a widely praised doctoral paper about the development of the sea spider. The promising young zoologist received a one-year fellowship to study at a famous zoological center in Naples, Italy.

Thomas Hunt Morgan

The late 1800s was a time of intense scientific discovery and debate. Biologists hoped to discover the chemical and physical manner in which organisms grow from single cells into fully formed animals. Morgan studied the work that German scientist Wilhelm Roux had done with the developing eggs of frogs. Roux had killed one of the first two cells of a growing frog egg. The half-embryo that remained did not die but grew into part of a frog.

Scientists were learning other things about eggs. German-American scientist Jacques Loeb showed that sea urchin eggs could be fertilized artificially with chemicals. This led to speculation that it might be possible to change the course of an organism's growth by chemical as well as by physical means.

In Naples, Morgan read about the work being done by other scientists who were studying inherited traits. For years, people had wondered what parts of plants or animals carried the features of the parents. One widespread theory held that something in the parents' blood performed this function in humans.

An Austrian monk named Gregor Mendel had published a remarkable paper about heredity in 1865. Mendel spent years growing and studying pea plants to find out whether there were rules or patterns of inheritance. He wondered why some traits that disappear in one generation can turn up again in later generations. He also wondered why some traits pass on, unchanged, but other traits seem to combine the parents' traits. Mendel's careful experiments led him to formulate his laws, or rules, of heredity.

Mendel said that when each parent contributes the same kind of factor (for example, blue eyes), and the two factors come together in their offspring, a consistent trait (blue eyes in this case) results. But if one parent gives a factor that is different from the other (for example, brown eyes), a hybrid (mixture) occurs. The hybrid plant or animal forms its own reproductive cells. The two different inherited factors can then form new combinations with another parent cell during mating. The result depends upon the traits given by each parent. In other words, independent factors determine hereditary traits. Organisms get two such factors, one from each parent, for each trait, such as the green or yellow color in peas.

Mendel also stated that some traits are dominant (controlling) while others are recessive. The dominant factor is stronger than the recessive, so it will determine the inherited trait. Mendel went on to predict the ratio (relative numbers) of different traits that he found when he studied new generations of plants. For example, in his pea plants, Mendel found ratios of 3:1 for dominant and recessive traits. When he raised crops of plants and counted the types that resulted, he found three dominant traits for every one recessive trait.

In addition to Mendel, Morgan read reports by the Dutch biologist Hugo de Vries, who had conducted experiments with flowers called primroses. De Vries had found primroses whose shape differed from the others. He called these changes mutations (from the Latin *mutare*—"to change") and studied them for 20 years to determine what caused such changes.

De Vries noted that mutations occurred in only one or a few parts of the new flowers, never in every part of the plant. He concluded that the traits of living things occur in separate units. (Later, in 1909, these units of heredity would be called genes.)

Many scientists thought that traits of inheritance were carried in parts of the cell called chromosomes. Chromosomes are long, coiled, threadlike substances located in the nucleus of plant and animal cells. In the 1870s, a German scientist, Walther Flemming, found that some material inside the cell nucleus absorbed a colored dye that was not absorbed by any other part of the cell. He called this cellular material *chromatin*, from a Greek word meaning color.

Another scientist, Walter Stanborough Sutton, added more knowledge about chromosomes. In 1902, Sutton said that chromosomes occur in pairs, with each member of the pair having a similar structure. Studying human cells, Sutton said that the 46 chromosomes should be regarded as 23 *pairs*. Sutton found that the sperm and egg cells that unite to form a new human being contain only half of the needed chromosomes—23 in all. When these cells join, the resulting cell again contains 46 chromosomes (23 pairs).

Between 1905 and 1908, two British scientists, William Bateson and R. C. Punnett, conducted new genetic experiments to test Mendel's work. They did not always get the same results Mendel got in his pea plant experiments. Bateson and Punnett said that factors for individual traits might not be independent, as Mendel thought. Perhaps certain traits were connected? That way, combined traits would be passed from parent to offspring together.

During this period of discovery in the life sciences, Morgan became a biology professor at Bryn Mawr College in Pennsylvania. By 1904, he was well known in his field, having written 80 scientific papers and two biology books. That year, he married Lillian V. Sampson, a talented graduate student in his biology class. A scientist herself, Lillian Sampson Morgan also studied cells and embryos.

Morgan became head of the experimental zoology department of Columbia University in 1904. He focused on the study of heredity, hoping to find out how traits are passed from one generation to the next. Having studied Mendel's conclusions, Morgan did not agree with all of them. Like other scientists of the time, Morgan also questioned the theory of evolution that had been proposed by British scientist Charles Darwin in the 1850s. During a sea voyage around the world, Darwin had studied plants and animals and had concluded that they evolved gradually over a period of centuries from very simple to complex organisms. Morgan and others wondered how changes could occur in living things, allowing them to adapt to challenging conditions through the centuries. No scientist had yet thoroughly explained how traits can be passed on with changes.

Morgan planned careful experiments in order to get information about mutations and to test the theory that certain traits were "linked" with other traits. But first, he had to decide what living things to use in his tests. If he grew peas, as Mendel had, he would have to wait a year to study each new generation. Mice, rats, and birds were sometimes used in experiments, but none of them suited Morgan's needs. Then, in 1908, he heard about some biological experiments using *Drosophila melanogaster*, tiny insects commonly called vinegar flies or fruit flies, which feed on very ripe bananas and other fruits.

Fruit flies seemed ideal for his genetic tests. Morgan could capture them by leaving a ripe banana near an open window. The 1/4-inch long flies were cheap to feed and easy to house in half-pint milk bottles. A female fly laid hundreds of eggs only two days after mating with a male fly. Within 10 to 15 days, the flies grew from eggs to adults. Morgan and his research team could breed about 30 generations every year. And the flies only had four pairs of chromosomes, making them easier to study.

As he collected flies, Morgan put them into glass bottles with bits of banana that had been boiled to kill any germs. The bananas were also sprinkled with yeast so that they would ferment, or spoil. This gave the fly room, as people called it, a distinct smell. Into the bottles with the flies and fruit, Morgan and his assistants placed strips of paper so that the flies would have more living spaces. Morgan cut this paper from letters he received.

His associates often said that although "the Boss" was kind and generous with his own money, he was extra careful with laboratory funds. Morgan looked for clever solutions, rather than more money, to solve many problems. In this, he resembled Enrico Fermi and Robert Goddard, both of whom conducted their early research with small budgets.

Soon, there were several generations of flies inside the milk bottles. Morgan hoped that certain traits of the flies would undergo mutation—change—resulting in flies that had traits different than normal. He exposed the insects to extreme heat and cold or gave them diets high in salt or sugar. But generations later, no mutations had occurred. Morgan had not been able to cause changes in the physical traits of the flies.

Using his microscope and magnifying glass, Morgan had studied thousands of *Drosophila*, all with red eyes, when he discovered the first white-eyed fly in April 1909. He recorded the big event in his research notebook: "In a pedigreed culture of *Drosophila* which had been running for nearly a year, through a considerable number of generations, a male appeared with white eyes."

Next, Morgan put this white-eyed fly in an empty milk bottle and added a newly hatched, red-eyed female, so that the flies could mate. After nine days, there were 1,237 new flies. Morgan put the flies to sleep with an anesthetic called ether. Then he picked up a magnifying glass to examine their eyes. All of the flies had the red eyes common to their species.

Morgan was determined to explain why the white-eyed trait had disappeared. Although he had often disagreed with Mendel, Morgan now wondered if Mendel had been correct in saying that reproductive cells carry two kinds of traits, dominant and recessive.

Morgan mated more flies. About 14 days after he mated the original white-eyed male with the red-eyed female, he had 4,252 newborn flies to study. Cautiously, Morgan checked every fly himself, to avoid any errors. For several hours, he picked up flies and examined their eye color.

Morgan found that the ratio of red eyes to white eyes was nearly 3:1—the ratio of dominant to recessive traits that Mendel had found in his pea plants. After years of publicly disputing Mendel's theories, Morgan now acknowledged that the Austrian may have been correct.

Morgan had verified some of Mendel's findings; now he had a new puzzle to solve. Of the red-eyed flies in his test, some were female and others were male. But every one of the white-eyed flies was male. Why had no female flies inherited white eyes?

Morgan guessed that the eye-color trait might be connected to the trait of maleness, with the two traits being located on the chromosome that contains information about heredity. In reaching these conclusions, Morgan recalled the recent experiments by Bateson and Punnett.

Morgan's research helped to answer questions about how pairs of chromosomes can pass on so many different traits from parents to offspring. Parts of the chromosomes must contain these different factors, many scientists thought. The Danish botanist Wilhelm Ludwig Johannsen had called these units *genes*, from a Greek word meaning "to give birth to." Nobody had yet seen a gene, because they can only be viewed through high-powered microscopes, which had not yet been invented. Some scientists doubted that genes existed.

After his experiments, Morgan concluded that genes were indeed located on chromosomes. He visualized them as running lengthwise along the chromosome, somewhat like a string of beads. Morgan then theorized that genes for the white-eye trait and maleness were found together, on the same chromosome. As long as the chromosomes remained undamaged, the two traits would be passed on together, said Morgan. They were linked. Morgan announced his theory of "linkage" in July 1910.

After further studies, Morgan identified the chromosome that contained these two traits in the fruit flies. He was the first person to designate which specific genes were located on specific chromosomes.

Morgan continued to breed flies. By 1912, he had found and studied 40 different mutations. These changed traits included bodies that were crooked and wings that were much smaller than usual. Other flies were yellow-colored instead of black.

The fly room was now a very busy place. The new generations of flies had to be fed, divided into bottles, counted, and listed. Normal flies were separated from those with mutations. Besides doing many of these things and supervising the lab, Morgan was still teaching. Colleagues described the tall, thin professor as enthusiastic and tireless. They also admired his open-mindedness, as when he admitted that he had been wrong about Mendel's theories.

Fortunately, Morgan now had some capable associates. Among them were Calvin Bridges, Hermann J. Muller, and Alfred H.

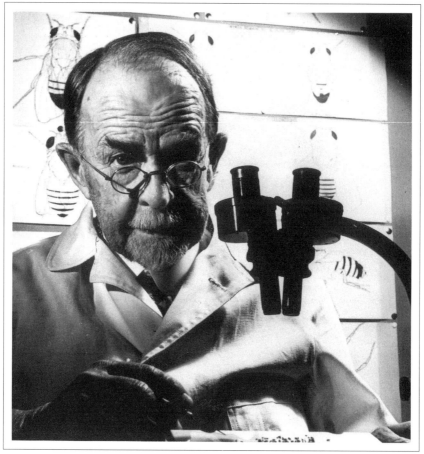

Morgan with microscope; pictures of Drosophila *can be seen on wall behind.*
(Courtesy of the California Institute of Technology)

Sturtevant, all of whom had begun as students under Morgan. These men went on to do their own outstanding work in genetics.

As the experiments went on, the fruit flies showed more surprising changes. Traits that had been inherited together became "unlinked." New combinations produced flies with stunted wings and yellow bodies, for example. Looking for explanations, Morgan reviewed the 1909 work of Danish biologist F. A. Janssen. Janssen had found that when cells are in the process of dividing, chromosomes sometimes get wrapped around each other, or they overlap. Morgan labeled this event a "crossing over." He reasoned that crossing over causes the chromosomes to break at the crossing point. The broken pieces then join together, but not in the same way as before. Loose pieces of different chromosomes lying next to each other become connected, so traits that once were linked to the same chromosomes can be passed on separately.

In 1913, Morgan published a "gene map" showing where different genes are located along the four pairs of chromosomes in *Drosophila*. He changed some gene locations in later years as his research showed new mutations and linkages in the flies. Morgan's chromosome map is viewed as a remarkable event in the history of biology.

By 1914, Morgan found more evidence to support his linkage theory. He also discovered that longer chromosomes held more traits than did the shorter chromosomes. This strengthened the idea that genes were positioned in rows on the chromosomes. Longer chromosomes would have room for longer rows of genes. Morgan gathered more evidence that accidental breakages in the chromosomes during cell division lead to the separation and repositioning of genes that once were linked.

Morgan, Sturtevant, Bridges, and Muller summarized their work in a book, *The Mechanism of Mendelian Heredity*, published in 1915. They restated Mendel's rules in light of new findings, including the theories of linkage and crossing over and data about the arrangement of genes along the chromosomes.

While at Columbia, Morgan bred thousands of flies and studied dozens of traits and mutations. During those years, it was often easy to recognize biology students from the university. They walked to and from school carrying bottles full of flies that had to be counted as part of the day's homework. Later, Alfred Sturtevant wrote about his experiences in the laboratory, saying, "There can have been few times and places in scientific laboratories with such an atmosphere of excitement and such a record of sustained enthusiasm."

In the meantime, Morgan had acquired another scientist in his lab: his wife, Lillian, who had spent 13 years away from research while rearing the couple's three daughters and a son. She, too, began to study *Drosophila*. One day Lillian Morgan found an odd female fly with several male traits. After breeding more of these flies, she developed a theory and wrote a highly regarded paper to explain how such a mixed-up insect had occurred.

In 1922, Morgan received the Darwin Medal, given for outstanding achievement in science. He became president of the National Academy of Science in 1927 and served at that post until 1931.

In 1928, Morgan moved across the United States to become head of Kerckhoff Biological Laboratories at the California Institute of Technology (Caltech) in Pasadena. At a reception given in his honor, Morgan said humorously, "Of course I expected to go to California when I died, but the call to come to the Institute arrived a few years earlier, and I took advantage of the opportunity to see what my future life would be like."

Morgan set up a biology department and a marine laboratory at Corona del Mar. He inspired other scientists at Caltech, including the brilliant chemist Linus Pauling. In the April 26, 1974, issue of *Nature* magazine, Pauling recalls how Morgan arrived at the institute "with a number of very able younger biologists." Says Pauling, "I began . . . to think about possible ways in which biological specificity could be explained in terms of interactions between

Morgan in his laboratory at Caltech in 1932. At his left are some specimen bottles; behind him are pictures of fruit flies on the wall.
(Courtesy of the California Institute of Technology)

molecules." This interest in biology sparked much of Pauling's later research.

Morgan made Caltech a prominent genetic research center. As before, his lab was filled with thousands of glass bottles housing flies. In 1930, he served as president of the American Association for the Advancement of Science; then in 1932 as president of the 6th International Congress of Genetics.

One day, the 67-year-old Morgan, still energetic, was at work among his fly bottles when he received a letter from Sweden. People in the lab reported that Morgan read the letter silently, then continued his work for several hours. Only after he finished his experiment did the scientist tell the others that he had won the 1933 Nobel Prize in physiology or medicine. It was the first time that a scientist born and trained in America had won a Nobel Prize in this field.

In Stockholm, Sweden, Morgan told the audience, "The whole subject of human heredity in the past has been so vague and tainted by myths and superstition that a scientific understanding of the subject is an achievement of the first order." Morgan credited his associates for their part in his achievements. He shared the $40,000 Nobel Prize money with Calvin Bridges and Alfred Sturtevant.

Morgan became emeritus professor of biology when he retired as head of his department at Caltech in 1941 at age 75. On Saturdays, he went to the Kerckhoff Marine Biological Station at Corona del Mar to collect specimens of the sea squirt (a small sea animal without a backbone that resembles a potato). Thomas Hunt Morgan did not stop working until he died on December 4, 1945, at age 79. His widow, Lillian Morgan, continued to make important findings until she died in 1952, at age 82.

Called the "grand old man of genetics" by biographer Bernard Jaffe, Morgan laid the groundwork for later scientists. His painstaking work enabled people to sort out what Morgan called the "myths and superstition" that once clouded the field of genetics. Morgan replaced them with facts and explanations, giving future geneticists the tools they needed to understand patterns of heredity and predict many of these patterns with greater accuracy than ever before.

Morgan once explained that he set out to "handle the problems of genetics on a strictly numerical basis." He achieved this and more, turning genetics into a real science—one that would lead to dramatic discoveries and practical uses in the 20th century.

Chronology

▬▬▬▬▬▬▬

September 15, 1866	Thomas Hunt Morgan born in Lexington, Kentucky
1886	receives B.S. degree in zoology from State College of Kentucky
1890	receives Ph.D. in biology from Johns Hopkins University in Baltimore, Maryland
1891	becomes biology professor at Bryn Mawr College
1904	becomes head of experimental biology department at Columbia University; focuses on the study of heredity
1908	begins using *Drosophila melanogaster* as the subject for his genetic experiments
1909	discovers a white-eyed male born to two red-eyed parent flies; conducts numerous breeding experiments; announces his theory of linkage in July
1912	has found and studied more than 40 different mutations; develops his theory of crossing-over
1913	publishes a gene map, showing the location of different genes along the four chromosomes of *Drosophila*
1915	*The Mechanism of Mendelian Heredity* is published; co-authored by Morgan, Bridges, Muller, and Sturtevant
1924	receives the Darwin Medal for outstanding achievement in science

1927	named president of the National Academy of Science (1927–31)
1928	becomes head of the department of biology at Caltech and remains on the faculty until his death in 1945; helps to establish the Marine Laboratory at Corona del Mar
1930	becomes president of the American Association for the Advancement of Science
1923	president of the 6th International Congress of Genetics
1933	awarded the Nobel Prize for physiology or medicine
1939	receives the Copley Medal given by the Royal Society of London
December 4, 1945	dies in Pasadena, California, at age 79

Further Reading

Jaffe, Bernard. *Men of Science in America*. New York: Simon and Schuster, 1958. A detailed profile of Morgan and his genetic experiments; includes diagrams of chromosomes.

Judson, Horace Freeland. *The Eighth Day of Creation: The Makers of the Revolution in Biology*. New York: Simon and Schuster, 1979. A history of the development of molecular biology and studies in genetics; discusses Morgan and his research.

Morgan, Thomas Hunt. *The Theory of the Gene*. New York: Hafner Publishing Co., Inc., 1964. Morgan's classic discussion of genetics, which became a well-known textbook. For older readers.

"Professor Thomas H. Morgan." Article, Columbia University, public relations department. Brief description of Morgan's work in the "fly room," from the institution at which he did his ground-breaking work.

Seidler, Ned and Rick Gore. "Seven Giants Who Led the Way." *National Geographic*, Vol. 150, No. 3 (September 1976), 401–407. Overview of landmark discoveries in biology, made by Leeuwenhoek, Darwin, Mendel, Pasteur, Morgan, and Watson and Crick.

Serafini, Anthony. *Linus Pauling: A Man and His Science*. New York: Paragon House, 1989. Mentions Morgan's influence on Pauling after the geneticist began teaching and conducting research at Caltech, where Pauling was a younger researcher and professor.

Albert Einstein: Creating the Thinking Tools of Modern Physics

A 1933 photo of Einstein riding a bicycle at his friend Ben Meyer's home.
(Courtesy of the California Institute of Technology)

*I*n 1905, a 26-year-old patent clerk living in Bern, Switzerland, made an astonishing announcement: matter and energy are essentially the same thing, but in different forms. Furthermore, matter can be changed into energy. In a handwritten paper that he submitted to a physics journal, the scientist expressed his idea

15

in a brief equation: $E = mc^2$. (Energy is equal to mass multiplied by the velocity, or speed, of light, squared.)

Scientists around the world read this amazing proclamation, which overturned long-held principles of physical science. Some laughed and rejected the idea; others worked to understand it; some criticized it strongly. Yet some 30 years later, the theory and equation were proven to be true. The atom was split, releasing energy in the process. And in 1945, the explosion of the world's first atomic bomb offered shattering proof of the notion that matter could be transformed into vast quantities of energy. On that day, a single ounce of plutonium produced the amount of explosive energy held in 20,000 tons of TNT.

The man who predicted that people could produce energy that did "not come from the sun" was Albert Einstein. Known as one of the great scientific geniuses of all time, he introduced many other important principles, such as the theory of relativity, that are basic to modern physics. Aside from his scientific contributions, Einstein was known as a fine person—kind, generous, and modest, with little interest in material things or publicity.

Albert Einstein was born in Ulm, Germany, on March 14, 1879. When he was one year old, his family left the southern German town, located on the Danube River, near the Swabian Alps. Both sides of his family had lived in southern Germany for more than a century, working as clerks, farmers, and merchants. They moved to Munich, where his father, Hermann Einstein, and his uncle Jakob operated a small factory that made electrical and technical supplies.

Einstein enjoyed a pleasant home life with his cheerful parents. His mother, Pauline Koch Einstein, shared her interests in music and poetry with Albert and his sister Maja, who was born in 1881. Einstein recalled being fascinated by a pocket compass at age five. He liked simple outdoor activities, such as watching birds and insects.

The Einstein family was Jewish, but as there was no Jewish school in their area, Albert attended a Catholic elementary school. Albert Einstein did not show signs of his later genius during those early years. He did not learn to talk as fast as other children. His parents worried about his shyness, his lack of friends, and his poor academic performance, especially in foreign languages. Einstein rebelled against rigid rules and did not like memorizing dates and lists or reciting answers that came straight from his textbooks. His teachers concluded that he was not intelligent.

At age 10, he had completed his elementary schooling and began attending the Luitpold Gymnasium (a secondary, or high school), which also required strict discipline. Einstein showed little enthusiasm for Latin or Greek and was known as a daydreamer who did not seem able to give back answers in the same way that he had been taught. Yet Einstein got encouragement from his family and close friends. He developed strong interests on his own. At age 12, he read a geometry book that excited him more than any previous academic subject. Einstein later wrote that geometry had aroused his sense of wonder and shown him the pleasure of learning. He began to think that people could "get certain knowledge of the objects of experience by means of pure thinking."

As he read other books, Einstein asked himself many questions. He was not satisfied with easy, commonly accepted answers. In geometry, he soon surpassed his classmates, as well as a medical student, Max Talmud, a family friend who ate dinner at the Einstein house on Thursday evenings. Talmud brought Einstein colorfully illustrated books about plants, animals, and astronomy. During those years, science was a popular subject in Germany, and many attractive science books were available. Einstein later recalled that as a 15-year-old, he enjoyed a set of books that described important scientific discoveries throughout history.

During his early teens, Einstein enjoyed playing the piano and violin. Once, he had practiced only because his mother insisted; now, he practiced on his own, later attributing this change of heart to a "love for Mozart sonatas." He often played to relax while studying difficult mathematical problems. Albert Einstein had managed to teach himself calculus and was hoping to pursue a career in science and mathematics.

Unfortunately, by 1894, Hermann Einstein's business had failed. Some relatives were doing well in Italy, so Hermann decided they would move to Milan. Einstein looked forward to living in Italy, with its sunnier climate and opportunity for boating on the coast. He was upset when his parents insisted that he stay in Munich to finish his schooling. Lonely and unhappy, Einstein disliked his impersonal school more than ever. He felt ill and tried to think of ways to leave. The school officials solved the problem by asking him to go, citing his apathy and his dislike for the school's methods.

Relieved, the 15-year-old Einstein joined his family, now living in Pavia, Italy. He visited his cousins in Genoa. Hermann Einstein told his son that he must now support himself because of the family's meager income. Einstein had not given up his dream of studying at a university, but now he had no money. The cousins in Genoa offered to support him if he could manage to live very simply. Einstein assured them he did not mind, so long as he could get the education he needed to become a teacher.

Einstein encountered another obstacle when he applied for admission at the prestigious Federal Institute of Technology in Zurich, Switzerland. By now, he had decided to study physics, especially the subjects of light, motion, and velocity. But Einstein failed the entrance examination. He did not know enough about natural sciences, such as zoology and botany, or languages. The director of the school praised Einstein's high scores in math and physics and advised the young German to spend a year at a secondary school in Aarau, a small town on the Aar River not far from Zurich. There, he could study the subjects he had failed.

Einstein preferred the schooling in Aarau to that which he had received in Munich. One teacher, Professor Winteler, invited Einstein to live at his home while enrolled at the school. His son, Karl, was Einstein's age, so the two boys became friends. And Frau Winteler was warm and motherly. After spending a successful year in the Swiss school, Einstein qualified for admission to the institute in 1896. Finally, he would be able to "answer questions about things I want to know," as he later put it.

Einstein appreciated the atmosphere and fine teachers at the Polytechnic Institute, among whom was a brilliant Russian-German mathematics professor, Hermann Minkowski. Here, Einstein was encouraged to ask questions. This fit more with his belief that the true purpose of learning was to gain understanding. He was liked by his fellow students, but the curly haired young man with the serious dark eyes did not spend much time socializing. He studied at every available opportunity, again pursuing subjects on his own.

Eventually, Einstein began to go out with friends, attending concerts or exhibits and discussing science, politics, and philosophy. His closest friends were often, like himself, living far from home. Einstein began dating a Hungarian physics student named Mileva Maric.

While attending the institute, he made an important decision: he renounced his German citizenship, believing that the freer Swiss political system and way of thinking were better. Einstein budgeted his small monthly allowance even more carefully, to save the money he would need to obtain a Swiss citizenship, which he could seek after living there for four years.

In July 1900, Einstein graduated from the institute and looked unsuccessfully for a teaching position. He was becoming discouraged when he was offered a temporary job teaching mathematics at a boys' school in Winterthur, northeast of Zurich. His students responded to his enthusiasm and ability to explain complex material clearly. Next, Einstein took another temporary job, teaching at the town of Schaffhausen.

After four years of being a "stateless person" (one with no citizenship), Einstein officially became a Swiss citizen in 1901. He hoped that his new status would help him find a teaching job. But a year later, he was still unemployed and worried about supporting himself. A friend, Marcel Grossman, told him about a job in the Federal Office of Patents in Bern. After an interview, Einstein was hired as a technical expert in the patent office. The job offered a steady income and time for his studies of physics.

In 1903, he married Mileva Maric. Maric had hesitated because she wanted to pursue an active physics career of her own. Once married, the couple settled into a small apartment. Einstein was pleased that Mileva and a few other close friends were knowledgeable about his favorite subject, physics, and were willing to discuss his new theories. That same year, he presented a paper to a group of scientists in Bern.

The subjects of light and motion absorbed Einstein's attention during those days. Many old scientific ideas were then being challenged by physicists around the world. In his solitary studies, Einstein, too, reexamined old theories. He began working on a new photoelectric theory. Scientists then knew that when a metal plate is exposed to a beam of light, it emits a shower of negatively charged particles (electrons). Nobody had explained why this happens. Einstein said that light is made up of individual particles of energy, rather than simply waves of energy. Other scientists had begun calling these particles quanta, but Einstein preferred to call them photons. He said that when these photons hit the metal plate, they bump into electrons that are at rest. They lend their energy to those they strike and "smack" them so that these electrons go through the metal plate.

Einstein further explained, with mathematical equations, how the speed at which the electrons exit the metal plate depends on the color of the light source being used: Photons of violet and ultraviolet light contain more energy than do red or infrared photons; thus, a violet or ultraviolet light causes electrons to be ejected at greater speeds.

As Einstein continued to work on this theory, his first son, Hans Albert, was born in 1904. Though offered permanent employment at the patent office, by 1905 Einstein had finished a paper detailing his theory about photoelectric effect. The editor of the scientific journal *Annals of Physics* accepted the article. It caused a stir among scientists who were not willing to give up the older theory that light was transmitted as waves.

During this year of amazing achievement, Einstein published another important paper, discussing Brownian movement. Robert Brown, a British botanist, had noticed that plant spores (reproductive bodies that usually contain only one cell) floating on the water are never at rest. These small particles move about in constant zigzag motions, increasing their activity when heat is introduced.

Scientists had long supposed that molecules, not visible at that time under a microscope, did exist. Yet nobody had proven this. Einstein wrote that molecules behaved exactly as the visible particles did, with the same kinetic energy (energy a body possesses as a result of its motion). Again, he used a series of carefully developed mathematical equations to support his theories. The article was accepted and published by *Annals of Physics* in 1905. Einstein showed how one could calculate the number of molecules in a unit volume by measuring the distances traveled or displaced by the visible particles in suspension.

But the work for which Einstein is best known was contained in his 1905 paper describing his theory of special relativity. Einstein had spent a great deal of time thinking about the relationships between space, time, and motion. He had also been analyzing these concepts in view of some experiments done in the 1880s by two American scientists, Albert Michelson and Edward Morley.

The famous British physicist Isaac Newton (1642–1727) had offered an explanation for the way in which light waves travel through space. Space must contain something, which scientists called an "ether"—a transparent, weightless material that surrounds the Earth and offers little or no resistance to the light passing through. To test this idea, Michelson and Morley conducted experiments to see whether a beam of light would travel faster when going in the direction of the Earth's movement or when traveling in the opposite direction. (This idea can be compared to the way in which a person swimming or rowing a boat can go faster traveling *with* the current than when going against it.)

For their experiment, Michelson and Morley measured the speed at which their light beams traveled in these two different directions. They found no difference in the speed. This cast a great deal of doubt on the idea that the Earth was surrounded by ether.

Einstein suggested a possible explanation. He said that the speed of light is constant—that it travels at the same velocity, regardless of the place it comes from. Einstein understood that if the speed of light is a constant in the universe, then old ideas about space, time, and motion would have to be revised. He went on to say that motion is always relative. There is no such thing as absolute motion or an absolute lack of any motion. It depends upon the velocity, time, and position of the observer to the event. He then concluded that time moves more slowly as one travels at speeds approaching the velocity of light. Following this idea, if a person traveled on a spaceship that moved at a rate close to the speed of light and returned to earth after several years, he or she would be only a few days older. But the people who stayed on earth and did not travel at such high speeds would be years older.

Exploring these ideas further, Einstein developed a theory that revised two other basic ideas of physics: the law of conservation of energy and the law of conservation of matter. The first states that the energy of interacting bodies or particles in a closed system remains constant. The second states that matter is neither created nor destroyed and that the total amount of matter in the universe always stays the same. Einstein declared that matter and energy are not separate and distinct; they are one entity in two separate states—matter being energy in a frozen state, and energy being matter in a fluid state.

Einstein provided a formula to describe the relationship between matter and energy: $E = mc^2$. According to this equation, a given amount of matter equals a definite amount of energy. This was a startling idea, for it claimed that vast quantities of energy were "frozen" in tiny amounts of matter. The formula said that energy (in terms of measurement units called ergs) contained in one gram of matter could equal the square of the velocity of light (measured at close to 186,000 miles/second or 30 billion centimeters/second). Thus, one gram of matter holds the equivalent of 900 billion ergs, or about 25,000,000 kilowatt hours. This is an incredible amount of energy—18,000 million times greater than that released by burning a gram of coal.

Einstein in 1905, the year he published his famous paper on the special theory of relativity. Then 26 years old, he was working as a patent clerk in Bern, Switzerland.
(Photo by Lotte Jacobi; courtesy of Argonne National Laboratory)

At the age of only 26, Albert Einstein submitted this theory of special relativity in a 30-page paper with few footnotes and no references to other experts. The paper, entitled "On the Electrodynamics of Moving Bodies," was published but did not bring its author immediate fame. Later experiments would verify many of his ideas. In the 1930s and 1940s, $E = mc^2$ would become a famous equation, after the atom was split and atomic weapons were made.

For now, Einstein's life stayed much the same. In 1906, he was promoted to a higher position at the patent office, with a small raise in salary. He published a paper on the specific heats of solid matter, the first paper ever written on the subject of quantum theory and solid states. Quantum theory originated with German physicist Max Planck in 1900. He studied heat radiation and theorized that the energy of vibrating electrons could not change continuously but changed in such a way that the energy of the system always stayed equal to a whole number of so-called energy-quanta. Solid-state physics is concerned with whether there is a free movement of electrons in a given substance. For example, metals (but not nonmetals) are characterized by a free movement of electrons. This field of physics grew after World War II with the discovery of transistors and superconductivity.

When scientists tested Einstein's earlier theories about the movements of molecules, they found that his formulas were correct. Recognizing his outstanding research and publications, the University of Zurich awarded Einstein a Ph.D. in physics.

It was not until 1909 that Einstein was asked to lecture on his theory of relativity in Salzburg, Austria, at a meeting of scientists. Now age 30, he was invited to become an associate professor at the University of Zurich. Within two years, he began to teach at the German University in Prague. A triumphant Einstein returned to Zurich as a full professor when he began teaching at the Institute of Technology in 1912.

World War I was approaching in 1914 when Einstein accepted an excellent offer to become director of the Kaiser Wilhelm Physical Institute in Berlin, Germany. There, he would be able to spend almost all of his time doing research. By then, he and Mileva had two sons, but their marriage was not happy. Mileva did not want to go to Germany, and they decided to separate.

In Berlin, Albert Einstein found that he was a celebrity. For the next 17 years, he was praised and respected by scientists and the general public. He received honorary degrees and appointments to important scientific societies, even though he publicly opposed World War I.

Einstein developed other revolutionary theories, this time about gravitation. He had long sought to explain why the orbit of the planet Mercury has shifted slightly in space through the years. Isaac Newton's laws of gravity stated that each planet follows an elliptical orbit path around the sun. The shift in Mercury's position (called a precission by scientists) did not follow the Newtonian laws. Einstein also noticed that acceleration can locally cancel out a gravitational force.

Using his new unified theory of gravitation, Einstein provided an answer: Newton had viewed gravity as a force that occurs between objects. Einstein said that gravity involved a space-time curvature, in which there was a gravitational bending of light around a massive object. The massive bodies of the stars and planets produce such curvings of light. Mercury is so close to the sun, said Einstein, that space-time affects it more—the curved space-time is stronger because of the sun's great mass. This idea was one part of Einstein's general theory of relativity. He said that the gravitational field of the sun bends the light emitted by stars, as well as affecting the orbit of the planet Mercury.

These new theories about gravitation were tested four years later by scientists at London's Royal Astronomical Society. On March 29, 1919, there was an eclipse of the sun. Teams of astronomers in Brazil and West Africa tested the general theory of relativity. With special cameras and equipment, they photographed the stars that came out around the sun in the dark sky during the eclipse. Then they measured the positions of the stars to see if their positions had shifted. That would show that light was indeed affected by gravity.

After studying pictures taken during the eclipse and comparing the measurements with those done on previously photographed maps of the sky, the astronomers found that the light rays were curved from their formerly straight paths because of the attraction of the sun. The gravitational field of the sun bent the light of the stars, as Einstein's general theory of relativity had predicted.

In June 1919, Einstein remarried. His new wife was his cousin Elsa Lowenthal, who joined him in Germany. Einstein achieved worldwide fame when he received the Nobel Prize for physics in 1921, awarded to him for his explanation of the photoelectric effect. Einstein gave the $45,000 prize money to his former wife, Mileva, who was raising their two sons.

On Einstein's 50th birthday, he received masses of gifts, greetings, and messages. But things changed drastically as the Nazis rose to power in the 1930s. The Nazi leader, Adolf Hitler, publicly blamed Jews for Germany's economic problems. He aroused fear and contempt toward Jews and other people he disliked, dismissing them from jobs in government, universities, and elsewhere. He took away their legal rights and enforced arbitrary discriminatory policies.

Einstein receiving the second Planck medal, along with Max Planck, who received the first, on June 28, 1929. (Courtesy of the American Institute of Physics, Niels Bohr Library, Fritz Reiche Collection)

Born Jewish, Einstein did not then practice a particular organized religion. He believed in God and claimed that God "reveals himself in the harmony of all being." He thought that people of all nations must learn to live together without war. Einstein was appalled by the bigotry and hatred of the Nazi regime.

Whereas Einstein had once been an acclaimed scientist, now the Nazis criticized him and his theories and burned his books.

Great Scientists

When Hitler became dictator of Germany, Albert and Elsa Einstein were returning by ship to Europe from a lecture trip at the California Institute of Technology. Einstein decided to resign from the Kaiser Wilhelm Institute, renouncing the German citizenship he had resumed in order to work there in 1915. In Germany, Nazis raided Einstein's apartment and summer home, seizing his property.

For several months, Einstein and his family lived in Belgium. They helped other refugees fleeing from Germany to find jobs and travel to safe countries. The king of Belgium had sent police to guard Einstein after hearing rumors that the Nazis planned to execute him. The Einsteins decided they could not remain safely in a country that bordered Germany.

In October 1933, the Einsteins went to the United States, where Einstein would spend five months in Princeton, New Jersey, at the Institute for Advanced Study. Upon his arrival, the famous scientist was met by reporters. Americans who saw his picture came to think of Albert Einstein as a brilliant man with unruly white hair who wore casual clothes and shoes with no socks and who liked to play the violin.

Einstein enjoyed his work in Princeton and accepted an offer to continue there. He and Elsa moved into a modest home. They continued to help other refugees, finding money and Americans who would sponsor these troubled people.

Einstein's new job suited his needs. He had a professorship for life but was free of regular teaching duties. He was asked to choose his own salary, but Einstein named a figure so low that the heads of the institute felt embarrassed, so they raised it.

Asked about his plans, Einstein told newspaper reporters, "As long as I have any choice, I will stay only in a country where political liberty, toleration, and equality of all its citizens before the law is the rule."

On August 2, 1939, while at his vacation home on Long Island, Albert Einstein met with two well-known Hungarian-born physicists, Leo Szilard and Eugene Wigner. They had come with an urgent request: Would Einstein sign a letter to President Franklin D. Roosevelt, warning him that German physicists had recently split the uranium atom and that it now seemed possible to develop a chain reaction that would lead to the production of terrifying, destructive weapons? American scientists working on nuclear power were convinced that President Roosevelt would listen to Einstein, the world's most prominent scientist. The letter said, in part:

> Sir: Some recent work by E. Fermi and L. Szilard, which has been communicated to me in manuscript, leads me to expect that the element uranium may be turned into a new and important source of energy in the immediate future. . . . This new phenomenon would also lead to the construction of bombs, and it is conceivable—though much less certain—that extremely powerful bombs of a new type may thus be constructed.

As Albert Einstein read the two typed pages, he was said to remark, "For the first time in history men will use energy that does not come from the sun." He signed his name at the bottom. On October 11, President Roosevelt received the letter personally from a man named Alexander Sachs. The signature "A. Einstein" caught his attention. President Roosevelt appointed an advisory committee to study the use of uranium. Soon, money was appropriated in increasingly large amounts to enable U.S. scientists to work on atomic energy. Laura Fermi, wife of physicist Enrico Fermi who played a key role in this project, later wrote, "Undoubtedly, Einstein was the best person to act as a link between scientists and government."

In 1940, Einstein became a U.S. citizen. Elsa had died of heart disease in 1936, so she could not share this moment. World War II escalated during the early 1940s. While Einstein worked at the Institute for Advanced Study on new theories, he also did government work on atomic energy. His stepdaughter Margot lived with him off and on during those years.

Einstein continued to see close friends with whom he discussed politics and philosophy, as well as science. He opposed wars as a way to solve conflicts, but he thought the Nazis, who were invading other countries and persecuting untold numbers of people, had to be stopped. Einstein helped to raise money for the Allies through bond drives, benefit concerts, and other efforts.

In 1945, when the atomic bomb was completed and was dropped on Hiroshima, Einstein expressed the despair and regret that many other scientists felt. He had predicted that such an event was possible but wished that history had been different, so that atomic power would be used only for peaceful energy. After Japan surrendered, Einstein said, "The war is won but not the peace." His concern led him to organize groups of scientists who urged the U.S. government to work toward international control of nuclear weapons.

Einstein meeting with members of the mathematics department at the Institute for Advanced Study in Princeton, New Jersey.
(Photo by Alan Richards; courtesy of the Institute for Advanced Study)

During the last 10 years of his life, Einstein tried to find a unified field theory, one that would relate the universal properties of energy and matter. He hoped to connect theories of electromagnetism and gravity, explaining them in one equation or mathematical formula. On weekday mornings, he would leave for work usually before 9 o'clock. He walked the mile and a half to his office regardless of the weather until his final years, when the institute sent a car and driver for him. He then would go to his two-room suite on the second floor. Einstein liked to work in the smaller room, meant as an assistant's office, not the larger room with its big desk and library. He analyzed mathematical equations and theories with a notepad resting on his lap.

Shortly after noon, he would return home. People sometimes stared when they recognized his wavy silver-white hair and baggy pants, familiar turtleneck sweater, and favorite old brown leather jacket. Einstein spent as little time as possible on clothing or other things he considered trivial, so that he could save more time for his work.

He spent afternoons in his small study at home. Sometimes he would play the piano or violin. Science writer William Laurence reports that Einstein's neighbors regarded him as a kind person who enjoyed meeting children, even taking time to help a child with an arithmetic lesson that had confused her at school.

Einstein knew that many people thought his work was too complicated for them to understand. Although a grasp of some of his theories and equations does require advanced knowledge, Einstein thought that the main ideas could be understood, if explained well. With his customary sense of humor, Einstein told his secretary how to respond when asked to explain the theory of relativity. He suggested that she say something like this: When a young man spends two hours with a pretty girl, it seems like just a minute. But if he were to sit on a hot stove for just a second it would seem to him like two hours. That's relativity.

Einstein did not achieve the unified field theory that he had worked toward for many years. But his research helped other scientists working on similar theories. They could move ahead without covering the same ground. Although some people once ridiculed relativity, modern developments in such fields as astronomy and space exploration continue to support Einstein's ideas.

Einstein's friends continued to appreciate him as a scientist and as a person. His biographer, Leopold Infeld, said that "whatever he might say would be the product of his own mind uninfluenced by the shrieks of the outside world."

In his seventies, Einstein wrote about human responsibility. In 1955, he said that humans must work for peace and justice in the world and try to be ethical in both small and large matters. He wrote:

In matters concerning truth and justice, there can be no distinction between big problems and small; for the general principles which determine the conduct of men are indivisible. Whoever is careless with the truth in small matters cannot be trusted in important affairs. This indivisibility applies not only to moral but also political problems; for little problems cannot be properly appreciated unless they are understood in their interdependence with big problems.

He also shared his ideas about the importance of human feelings: "The most beautiful and profound emotion we can experience is the mystical. It is the source of all true art and science. He to whom emotion is a stranger, who can no longer pause to wonder and stand rapt in awe, is as good as dead; his eyes are closed."

When asked about his working methods, Einstein replied, "I grope."

People who got to know this human side of the famous physicist viewed him as a philosopher as well as a scientist. Although he suffered from illnesses of the digestive system during 1955, he told his friends that he still worked every day, claiming, "I am always working on something new."

After a brief illness, Albert Einstein died on April 18, 1955, at age 76. His son Hans and stepdaughter Margot were in Princeton at the time. He had agreed that his brain could be studied by scientists after his death but requested that his body be cremated without any fanfare afterward.

In a 1954 tribute to Einstein, Robert Oppenheimer had said, "The remarkable thing has been the wonderful eye that he has for the deep order of things—the immense power to get rid of the trivia, to see where the wide and beautiful truth lies." After his death, tributes came from around the world as people searched for words to describe Einstein's life and achievements.

During his youth, Albert Einstein had been labeled "slow," a failure in school who could not pass his first university admissions tests. He had struggled against poverty, unemployment, bigotry, and political turmoil. Yet when he died, people praised him as a person of immense talent who foresaw the atomic age and who laid the groundwork for 20th-century physics. Now, as the 21st century approaches, many people still regard Albert Einstein as the greatest scientist of all time.

Chronology

▬▬▬▬▬

March 14, 1879	Albert Einstein born in Ulm, Germany
1894	fails entrance examination for Polytechnic Institute in Zurich, Switzerland
1896	after an additional year of schooling, he passes the exam and is admitted to the institute
1900	receives degree in physics and mathematics; finds temporary teaching jobs
1902	begins working as a patent clerk in Bern
1905	publishes five important papers in *Annals of Physics*
1906	publishes paper on specific heats of solid matter, the first to apply quantum theory to solid-state physics
1909	becomes professor at the University of Zurich
1912	named full professor at the university
1914	becomes director of Kaiser Wilhelm Institute in Berlin, Germany
1921	awarded the Nobel Prize in physics, for his explanation of the photoelectric effect
1929	receives the Planck medal
1933	leaves Germany to live in United States, begins work at the Institute for Advanced Study in Princeton,

	New Jersey; serves as director until 1949
1939	signs letter urging President Roosevelt to support scientific research in nuclear energy, which led to the Manhattan Project to build the atomic bomb
1940	becomes U.S. citizen
1945	leads efforts for world peace, including the formation of groups of scientists to advocate international control of nuclear weapons
1947	resigns as director of Institute for Advanced Study but continues research, focusing on the development of a unified field theory
April 18, 1955	dies in Princeton, New Jersey, at age 76

Further Reading

Apfel, Necia H. *It's All Relative: Einstein's Theory of Relativity*. New York: Lothrop, Lee and Shepard, 1981. Diagrams and photographs help to explain the basic concepts of Einstein's theories. Includes demonstrations, as well as the thought experiments Einstein used when developing his ideas.

Asimov, Isaac. *Understanding Physics*. New York: Dorset Press, 1988. Introduction to the history and major theories of physics, in three volumes: *Motion, Sound, and Heat; Light, Magnetism, and Electricity; The Electron, Proton, and Neutron*.

Calder, Nigel. *Einstein's Universe*. New York: Viking, 1979. A description of Einstein's theories, the way they have changed humankind's view of the world, and their impact on modern physics.

Cuny, Hilaire. *Albert Einstein: The Man and his Theories*. London: Souvenir Press, 1961. A comprehensive biography with family photos and a glossary.

Fisher, David E. *The Ideas of Einstein*. New York: Holt, Rinehart, and Winston, 1980. Describes Einstein's theories of special and general relativity clearly for young readers.

Hunter, Nigel. *Albert Einstein*. New York: Franklin Watts, 1987. Illustrated story of Einstein's life and work for grades 5–8.

Lanczos, Cornelius. *Albert Einstein and the Cosmic World Order*. New York: John Wiley and Sons, Inc., 1965. Shows the connections between Einstein's theories and other important scientific movements.

Pais, Abraham. *Subtle Is the Lord: The Science and Life of Albert Einstein*. New York: Oxford University Press, 1982. Written by a physicist, this book explores Einstein's life and work in depth. For older readers.

Weaver, Jefferson Hane. *The World of Physics: Volume II: The Einstein Universe and the Bohr Atom*. New York: Simon and Schuster, 1987. A history of physics with essays by leading physicists. Volume II describes major discoveries in the late 19th and early 20th centuries and includes five of Einstein's papers, on the subjects of relativity, gravity, motion, and radiation.

Robert Hutchings Goddard: Launching America into Space

Goddard beside one of his rockets in his workshop at Roswell, New Mexico, about 1935.
(Courtesy of the Smithsonian Institution)

*T*he rocket was positioned inside a metal launching frame made from pipes. Although the sun shone that March day in 1926, snow covered the pasture where the rocket frame stood. The rocket was a slender device about 10 feet high. The tall, mustachioed man who had built it was a physics professor from Worcester, Massachusetts. His stood beside his invention as his wife photographed the historic event.

It was time to test the rocket. After years of research, the professor thought he had devised the right fuel to thrust a vehicle without propellers into the sky. The fuel was gasoline mixed with liquid oxygen—dangerous stuff, five times more powerful than the explosive TNT. An assistant, Henry Sachs, lit an igniter on the rocket, from which black smoke curled up. The professor pulled the release cord. The other assistant, Percy Roope, stood ready to measure the rocket's flight.

The crucial moment had come: Would the rocket fly or would it explode? All four people stood watching as flame shot out from the nozzle. With a faint roar, the rocket rose from its frame. The rocket had not exploded—it was soaring. After flying for about three seconds, it fell 184 feet from the launch site.

Compared to the rockets of today, this one had a limited flight: It climbed just 41 feet and traveled at a top speed of 60 miles per hour. But the first liquid-fuel rocket, launched in a field near Auburn, Massachusetts, was a vital step in what is now called the space age. The man who designed the rocket and developed principles for rocket flight is honored as America's first space scientist: Robert Hutchings Goddard.

Robert Goddard was born on October 5, 1882, in Worcester, Massachusetts. He was the only child of Nahum and Fannie Goddard, both descendants of families that had lived in New England since the 1600s. When Robert was less than one year old, the family moved to Boston where Nahum Goddard became co-owner of a shop that manufactured knives for machines.

With no brothers or sisters at home, Goddard spent many hours reading or playing alone. He explored the insides of clocks and other household gadgets. Nature fascinated him, too. He had many questions about the planets and the weather. Outdoors, he inspected spiders, worms, and frogs.

Frequent colds, coughs, and stomach illnesses kept Goddard out of school for months at a time. But his strong curiosity and encouragement from his parents helped him to learn at home. Nahum bought his son a set of books called *Cassell's Popular Educator* and the more difficult *Cassell's Technical Educator*. He provided equipment for Robert's many interests: a telescope for gazing at stars and planets, a microscope for examining bugs, art supplies for sketching and painting, a piano, even a typewriter (rarely found in homes during those days) for his stories and poems.

Goddard's chemistry experiments began at an early age. Once, he caused an explosion in the attic while trying to make artificial diamonds from hot graphite, oxygen, and hydrogen. His parents warned him to be more careful, but they did not forbid future experiments.

Unfortunately, Goddard's mother was also in poor health. She had tuberculosis, a lung disease that was then incurable. In 1899, her doctor suggested that country air might help, so the family returned to Worcester to live with Goddard's grandmother.

In spring 1899, Goddard was a thin 16-year-old who had finished only one year of high school. He had not received high grades, particularly in mathematics, a subject he sometimes disliked. He had curiosity and intelligence but no clear career goals.

Shortly after the family arrived at "Gram's" farm, Goddard became sick again and missed another year of school. While resting, he spent hours reading. One favorite book was *The War of the Worlds*, by British author H. G. Wells. Travel in outer space is described in this science fiction story.

On October 19 of that year, Goddard had an experience that shaped the rest of his life. He felt well enough to do light work in the yard. While trimming limbs high in a cherry tree, he had what he later described as a powerful daydream. Goddard stared at the sky and pictured himself soaring in space. In a brief autobiography, he later wrote: ". . . I imagined how wonderful it would be to make some device which had even the possibility of ascending to Mars."

When he left the tree, Goddard had chosen his life's work: to explore space. Although space exploration is now taken for granted, in 1899 most people thought the idea was ridiculous. The Wright Brothers had not yet flown their airplane at Kitty Hawk, North Carolina. That thrilling event would take place four years later, in 1903. People had flown in balloons that carried bags of "lighter-than-air" gases—but no higher than 28,000 feet. And the two French balloonists who reached that height in the 1860s died from the lack of oxygen.

Even so, Goddard thought that there must be a way to send a machine into the upper atmosphere, even to the moon. As he planned his career in science, education took on a new importance.

School had to wait, however. The doctor urged Goddard to rest at home for another year. During that time, he read scientific materials, observed the sky through his telescope, and examined the way birds used their wings in flight. He resolved to master both mathematics and physics when he returned to school.

In 1901, Goddard entered Worcester South High School as a sophomore. The tall, thin 19-year-old made friends quickly. He was elected to class offices, wrote for the yearbook, and played the piano at dances. He also excelled in mathematics—the results of his efforts to apply every concept he learned. "Any proposition I could think of, I would try to prove," he later wrote. He continued this practice all his life as he studied theories then devised experiments and machines to test them.

In June 1904, senior Robert Goddard presented one of two graduation speeches. He ended by saying, "It has often been proved true that the dream of yesterday is the hope of today and the reality of tomorrow."

Goddard was still recording ideas about space travel in his journal. He had built several flying devices, but none soared as he hoped. Still, as he wrote years later, ". . . though I reasoned with myself that the thing was impossible, there was something inside me that simply would not stop working."

That autumn, Goddard entered Worcester Technical Institute with the help of a loan. The Goddards were not poor, but medical bills and home care for Robert and his mother had left them without enough money for college tuition. Goddard studied engineering, physics, chemistry, and astronomy, while tutoring to earn money. In his spare time, he conducted experiments, recording his theories and computations in a set of cloth-bound notebooks. These notebooks held an ongoing account of his work during the next 10 years and are now part of the Goddard Collection at Clark University Library.

While at Worcester, Goddard decided that rockets were the most promising vehicle for space travel. Balloons and airplanes need oxygen to fly, but there is no oxygen in the upper atmosphere, which begins about 100–200 miles above the Earth's surface. At that level, the air becomes increasingly thin until there is a vacuum—airless space. The moon is 240,000 miles from Earth, so almost all that distance is a vacuum.

Goddard had seen rockets in fireworks displays at Fourth of July celebrations. He knew that the Chinese had been making rockets with gunpowder—solid fuel—for centuries, both for festivals and for combat. He also understood the scientific basis of rocket flight, expressed in the theories of British scientist Sir Isaac Newton

(1642–1727). Newton's Third Law of Motion, stated simply, says, "For every action there is an equal and opposite reaction."

Newton's Third Law can be demonstrated by filling a toy balloon with air. Inside the closed balloon, air exerts force against all the sides. But if the stem is opened, air streams out, and the balloon flies across the room. In a rocket, fuel is burned inside a hollow chamber, producing hot gases. When these gases expand and rush out of the rocket's nozzle, it flies upward—in the opposite direction of the escaping gases.

In 1909, Goddard began doctoral studies in physics at Clark University. During that time, he considered the use of liquid fuel to power a space-bound rocket. Liquid fuels would be easier to control, since the flow could be increased or decreased. They would also provide more power than an equal weight of powder fuel. Besides, a rocket would need to carry its own oxygen, cooled into a liquid, into space where no oxygen was present. Oxygen was needed for combustion—the burning of fuel inside the engine.

Goddard made other notes about a "combination rocket" (later called a multistage rocket). A single rocket with a heavy fuel tank would weigh too much to maintain enough speed to break out of the Earth's field of gravity (about seven miles per second, according to Goddard's calculations). But two rockets could be stacked together, he reasoned. Each would have its own engine, pumps, propellant tank, and control system. The first rocket would propel the craft up, then fall off after its fuel had burned. A smaller second stage would continue upward, soaring faster without the heavy first stage and because the force of gravity grows weaker at higher altitudes. About 1,600 miles above the Earth, the pull of gravity is only half as strong as it is near the surface.

After receiving his Ph.D. in 1911, Goddard began to teach at Clark. The next year, he accepted a research fellowship at Princeton University. Goddard was working long hours in his laboratory there when he developed an intense, persistent cough. Back home in Worcester, doctors diagnosed a life-threatening case of tuberculosis.

Confined to bed, Goddard used his research notes to make drawings, along with descriptions of rockets he planned to build. He applied for government patents for his liquid-fuel concept and for the combination rocket.

After Goddard became well enough to resume teaching at Clark, he devised laboratory experiments to show that a rocket could travel in a vacuum. By pumping air out of ceiling-high lengths of tubing, Goddard made a nearly airless space in which he fired small rockets. As he anticipated, the rockets traveled faster in the tube than they did in the atmosphere.

Goddard wanted to make a liquid-fuel rocket, but he did not have enough money for equipment. His small salary gave him just enough to support himself. In 1916 Goddard applied for a research grant from the Smithsonian Institution in Washington, D.C. His application included a 69-page paper called "A Method of Reaching Extreme Altitudes." Goddard proposed to build a rocket motor strong enough to climb 35 miles with a cargo of instruments.

The scientists who considered the proposal were intrigued: Such a rocket might be used to study and predict the weather. The Smithsonian granted him $5,000, and Goddard was able to continue his research.

Goddard's work changed course in 1917. For months, newspapers had reported the sinking of U.S. ships in the Atlantic by German U-boats. Now, the United States was entering World War I. In 1918 the Army Signal Corps asked Goddard to design combat weapons, so he moved to Pasadena, California, with his staff and equipment.

That November, Goddard went to the Aberdeen Proving Ground in Maryland to demonstrate a light-weight, portable weapon he had made: a solid-fuel rocket launched from inside a tube. The rocket blasted without a recoil that would injure the user. Army leaders planned to produce the weapon, but the war ended two days later. During World War II, Goddard's recoilless rifle was developed into the bazooka—a tube-launched weapon used to destroy tanks.

His war work ended, Robert Goddard returned to Clark University. The 37-year-old balding professor was teaching and conducting research when his life was disturbed in January of 1920. Never one to seek public attention, he now became the subject of embarrassing newspaper stories. The unwanted publicity occurred after the Smithsonian Institution published "A Method of Reaching Extreme Altitudes." Ignoring the scientific material, journalists focused instead on the few sentences Goddard had written about the possibility of sending a rocket to the moon.

Goddard was criticized and ridiculed throughout the country, by the public and the press. He was called a "crackpot" and "the Moon Man." In an editorial called "A Severe Strain on Credulity," a *New York Times* writer attacked Goddard's claim that rockets could travel in a vacuum, and also wrongly claimed that Goddard "does not knew the relation of action to reaction."

"From that day, the whole thing was summed up in the public mind in the word 'moon-rocket,' " Goddard later wrote. At first he tried to explain his ideas to the press. Eventually, though, he chose to ignore his critics, concentrating again on research.

One happy event during those years was Goddard's growing relationship with Esther Christine Kisk. Esther worked as secretary to the president of Clark University. At last, Goddard had found someone who cared about his well-being and his life's work. They were married in June 1924.

That year Goddard was also appointed head of Clark's physics department. In the laboratory, he tested flammable mixtures of liquid fuels and designed rocket engines. He searched for a pump material that could tolerate the low temperature of liquid oxygen.

Goddard standing next to the first liquid-fuel rocket, which he built, on March 16, 1926.
(Courtesy of Mrs. Robert H. Goddard and Goddard Space Flight Center; official NASA photo)

He also tried different positions for the engine and nozzle—the opening through which the gases escape.

Years of hard work resulted in the launching of the world's first liquid-fuel rocket on March 16, 1926. The site was a farm owned by Effie Ward, located three miles from Worcester near Auburn, Massachusetts. By mid-afternoon, the rocket had achieved its brief but historic flight.

Goddard ran to the cabbage patch to retrieve the wreckage. As he examined the pieces, he envisioned larger rockets that would reach higher altitudes. But he was pleased that this small rocket had flown—it meant that his engine worked. In a letter to a friend, Goddard wrote that the test "proved conclusively the practicality of the liquid propelled rocket."

After more tests, Goddard launched a rocket with a small cargo of instruments—what is now called a scientific payload. This 11 ½ foot rocket weighed about 32 pounds when empty. It carried a thermometer and a barometer (to measure atmospheric pressure), as well as a miniature camera to photograph the readings on the other instruments.

The rocket was tested on July 17, 1929, again at the Ward farm. Unlike previous tests, this one caused a commotion. The rocket roared loudly as it began its 90-foot ascent. It traveled a distance of 171 feet, then dropped to the ground.

Alarmed by the noise, people thought that an airplane had crashed and caught fire. They called the police and fire departments. Newspaper reporters rushed to the farm. Again, Goddard endured unpleasant publicity. "Moon Rocket Misses Target by 238,799 ½ miles," joked one headline.

The famous aviator, Colonel Charles Lindbergh, read about Goddard's work. Lindbergh had made history two years before when he flew an airplane, *The Spirit of St. Louis*, alone across the Atlantic Ocean. Lindbergh was impressed by Goddard and offered to get financial help for the scientist. He met with a friend, philanthropist Daniel Guggenheim, and showed him "moving pictures" that Esther Goddard had taken of the July launch. In December, Lindbergh called Goddard with good news: The Guggenheim Foundation would grant him $50,000 during the next two years.

The news came at an important time. The fire marshal had forbidden Goddard to launch any more rockets in Massachusetts. And although he had budgeted carefully, borrowing

*Goddard and colleagues holding the rocket used in the flight of
April 19, 1932.*
(Courtesy of Mrs. Robert H. Goddard and Goddard Space
Flight Center; official NASA photo)

equipment or hand-making it whenever possible, the Smithsonian funds were gone.

Goddard needed a warm, sparsely populated area where he could test larger rockets. He chose Roswell, New Mexico—". . . the most promising location, both in climate and terrain," he wrote in his journal. In 1930, the Goddards moved to Mescalero Ranch, along with their research team and equipment. Goddard supervised the building of a machine workshop and two launching towers.

In New Mexico, Goddard and his team made steady progress. The year ended with an impressive flight: one rocket soared to an altitude of 2,000 feet and reached a speed of 500 miles per hour—quite an advance over the flight four years earlier.

Although many tests ended in failure, progress continued during the next two years. Goddard developed a larger, stronger motor. He found a way to keep the walls of the combustion chamber cool. He also improved rocket stability. Earlier rockets tipped and crashed when they did not stay on course. Goddard finally solved that problem by installing a device containing a gyroscope that would control guiding vanes on the rocket. The vanes could regulate the gas streaming out of the nozzle. This light-weight gyroscope and the vanes helped Goddard to steer his rockets.

In autumn 1931, Goddard tested a remote-controlled rocket, and in 1935, one of his rockets climbed to nearly 7,500 feet. As 1936 arrived, Goddard finally received favorable publicity when reporters described his "greatest rocket." More people heard about his successful tests, and scientists from other countries asked for details. For more than 10 years, German scientists had obtained information about Goddard's work from Smithsonian

Goddard and colleagues at a test site at Roswell, New Mexico, on May 19, 1937. He is holding the cap and pilot parachute after a successful test.
(Courtesy of Mrs. Robert H. Goddard and Goddard Space Flight Center; official NASA photo)

publications and the United States Government Patent Office. The German government had begun sponsoring rocket research in 1932.

Goddard had often tried to get U.S. government support for rocketry. Now he worried that other countries, especially Germany, would develop rocket weapons they could use against America. But U.S. officials still showed little interest.

Goddard had long sought the right kind of pumps, once saying, "Both theory and common sense dictate that the total rocket weight be made up chiefly of fuel, and that the structure be as light as possible." During the early 1940s, he designed lighter pumps from aluminum.

When World War II began, navy leaders asked Goddard to work on military rockets. But the United States had made a late start. When the Japanese bombed Pearl Harbor on December 7, 1941, America had no rocket weapons.

In Germany, enthusiasm for rocketry led to the development of the V-2. (*V* stood for *Vergeltung*—or vengeance.) The V-2 was a 12-ton, 46-foot-long rocket that could soar 60 miles high and fly as fast as 2,550 miles per hour, thus escaping anti-aircraft weapons. In 1944, Germany launched V-2s from hidden sites in France. More than 1,000 long-range V-2s were used to attack England. They destroyed buildings, killed over 2,500 people, and injured thousands more.

Later, Goddard and his team examined diagrams of the V-2 and saw startling similarities to Goddard's designs. After the war, German space scientists who immigrated to America admitted using Goddard's ideas in their research.

Despite weakening health, Goddard worked for the navy in Annapolis, Maryland, to help develop a rocket that could be used on fighter planes, giving them a fast "jet-assisted" take-off. He designed a motor with a variable range of speed. This system let a pilot control the fuel—speeding the flow or slowing it, so that an aircraft could idle, then accelerate quickly. The design was used in later rockets that exceeded the speed of sound.

Goddard was working long hours. His cough worsened and he had difficulty speaking. Doctors diagnosed cancer of the larynx. Throat surgery did not stop the disease. During the week after surgery, Goddard felt well enough to write some notes for yet another patent application—in all, he was issued 214 patents for his ideas. Then, on August 10, 1945, at age 62, Robert Goddard died.

Belated honors came to America's first space scientist. His widow was given the Congressional Gold Medal and the prestigious Langley Medal for aerodromics. In 1959, the National Aeronautics and Space Administration (NASA) established the Goddard Space Flight Center in Greenbelt, Maryland. Exhibits of Goddard's work have been placed in the Smithsonian Institution and at the Roswell Museum in New Mexico. Congress ordered that a gold medal be minted in 1959 to commemorate Goddard's "pioneering research in rocketry."

In 1960, the estate of Robert Goddard received $1,000,000 from the U.S. government "for rights to use over 200 of Dr. Goddard's patents which cover basic inventions in the field of rockets, guided missiles, and space exploration."

"Every liquid-fuel rocket that flies is a Goddard rocket," said Dr. Jerome C. Hunsaker, a well-known rocket scientist. Other scientists agreed. After examining Goddard's patents in 1950, Dr. Wernher von Braun, the brilliant German scientist who came to head the U.S. space program after World War II, said, "Goddard was ahead of us all." He called Goddard his "boyhood hero."

Goddard's rare ability to put theory into practice set him apart from other purely theoretical rocket pioneers working elsewhere. Describing her husband's contribution in 1964, Esther Goddard wrote: "First, the orderly beauty of mathematics was used to supply proof of a possibility. Then, in the laboratory and the field, the intuitions of the research scientist . . . bridged the gap between theory and reality and laid down general lines upon which technicians and engineers could build."

A few months before he died, Robert Goddard speculated about future uses of rockets and jet planes. In an interview for the *Worcester Telegram*, he said, "I feel we are going to enter an era comparable in its progress to that in which the airplane advanced . . . I think it's fair to say you haven't seen anything yet. . . ."

Since the days of Goddard's almost solitary research, America has supported space exploration with laboratories, testing sites, and billions of dollars. When the Soviet Union became the first nation to launch a satellite, *Sputnik I*, into orbit in October 1957, U.S. efforts intensified. Competition between the two countries became known as the space race.

As with nuclear energy, rockets have been developed for both peaceful and military purposes. Space satellites have sent back useful information about the weather and the Earth's surface.

They have photographed planets such as Venus, Jupiter, Mars, and Saturn.

On July 6, 1969, 24 years after Goddard's death, *Saturn 5* was launched at Cape Canaveral. The 363-foot-long three-stage rocket carried nearly 6,500,000 pounds of liquid fuel. Onlookers, including Esther Goddard, watched the rocket take off with three astronauts inside. On July 20, astronaut Neil Armstrong became the first person to walk on the moon.

Although Goddard did not live to see the moon landing he had imagined, he did see the destructive use of rockets in the form of the V-2. Just as energy released from the splitting of the atom gave the world new powers to destroy human life or enhance it, so it was with the rocket. In *This High Man*, Goddard biographer Milton Lehman considers Goddard's possible response to these developments:

> *Perhaps at the end, Goddard could have foretold that the major difference between the ballistic missile . . . and the space vehicle . . . lay not so much in their thrusts nor in their angles of departure, but in the nature of man. At one angle of ascent, the rocket was a weapon, at another a space craft. With a nuclear payload carried forward, it would become the most devastating of weapons and weapon carriers; with nuclear energy transported to its rear, it would become the greatest of all prime movers devised by man.*

Chronology

October 5, 1882	Robert Hutchings Goddard born in Worcester, Massachusetts.
1899	visualizes a vehicle that would enable people to travel in outer space
December 17, 1903	a heavier-than-air, engine-powered aircraft is successfully launched and piloted by the Wright Brothers
1904	Goddard enters Worcester Technical Institute
1909	begins doctoral studies at Clark University
1911	after receiving a Ph.D. in physics, Goddard begins teaching
1914	receives U.S. patent for idea of multi-stage rocket
1916	awarded grant from the Smithsonian, after submitting a scientific paper, "A Method of Reaching Extreme Altitudes"
1918	asked by U.S. Navy to design combat weapons
1920	ridiculed in the press for his Smithsonian paper
1924	appointed head of physics department at Clark; conducts experiments with liquid fuels and rocket engines
March 16, 1926	launches the first liquid-fueled rocket
July 17, 1929	launches the first rocket carrying a scientific payload of instruments
1930	moves to Roswell, New Mexico, to build laboratory and workshops and to test larger rockets

1930–41	builds and tests various rockets and their components
1932	uses vanes in a rocket motor blast for guidance; develops a gyro control device for rockets
1935	fires a liquid-fuel rocket faster than the speed of sound
1941	begins work for U.S. government on military rockets and fighter plane components
August 10, 1945	dies at age 62

Further Reading

American Heritage Magazine. *Men of Science and Invention*. New York: Harper and Row, 1960. Profile of Robert Goddard, along with other famous scientists.

Asimov, Isaac. *How Did We Find Out About Outer Space?* New York: Walker and Company, 1977. Part of a series of books that discuss scientific concepts and discoveries in clear, understandable text.

Clarke, Arthur C., and the editors of *Life. Man and Space*. New York: Time-Life Books, 1964. Includes an introduction written by Esther Kisk Goddard, the scientist's widow.

Davis, Watson. *The Century of Science*. New York: Duell, Sloan and Pearce, 1963. Includes a profile of Goddard, discussing his contributions to rocketry and space flight.

Faber, Harold and Doris. *American Heroes of the 20th Century*. New York: Random House, 1967. A brief biographical sketch of Goddard, describing his major achievements; includes photographs.

Goddard, Mrs. R. H. "Rocket Man." *Saturday Evening Post*, Vol. 226, No. 6 (June 12, 1954): 6. Goddard's widow discusses his life and work.

Goddard, Robert H. "Autobiography: R. H. Goddard." In Arthur C. Clarke, ed., *The Coming of the Space Age*. New York: Meredith Press, 1967. A brief autobiography of the scientist, discussing his early life and years of effort to develop successful rockets.

———. *Rocket Development*. Edited by Esther C. Goddard and G. Edward Pendray. New York: Prentice-Hall, 1948. A scientific and technical work by Goddard, with diagrams.

Lehman, Milton. *This High Man*. New York: Farrar, Straus and Company, 1963. A comprehensive, well-documented biography of the scientist.

Siry, J. W. "Rocket Research in the Twentieth Century." *Science Monthly*, Vol. 71 (December 1950): 408–21. Discusses Goddard's important contributions to early rocketry and its later development.

Arthur Holly Compton:
Cosmic and Atomic Quest

Arthur H. Compton.
(Courtesy of Argonne National Laboratory)

At the turn of the century, scientists studying radiation came upon what they regarded as one of the great mysteries of the universe. Using instruments designed to test the radioactivity of various elements, they noticed that their Geiger counters and other devices recorded levels of radiation even when substances such as radium were not around. The scientists did not know where this radiation came from, but they decided that rather than coming from the Earth itself it came from elsewhere in the cosmos. Thus they named these invisible forces cosmic rays.

Today, satellites and other sophisticated instruments are sent miles beyond the Earth to study cosmic rays, the high-speed

50

particles that are released when the nuclei of atoms from outer space collide. But in 1930 when physicist Arthur Compton developed a large-scale program to study cosmic rays, his tools were much simpler. He circled the globe for three years to conduct "Compton's survey," using a type of electroscope that he had devised. His goal was to measure the intensity of cosmic rays at different times of the year and at altitudes ranging from sea level to mountaintops.

Scientists from many parts of the world participated in Compton's study, working in one of the eight zones into which the Earth had been divided. Recording devices were placed at the top of Mount McKinley in Alaska and aboard an ocean liner that cruised between British Columbia and Australia, among other sites.

An ex-football player, the tall, ruggedly built scientist learned mountain climbing for his research. At Mount El Misti near Arequipa, Peru, he climbed 19,200 feet. Compton also used the hours he spent aboard airplanes taking pictures he hoped would give more clues about cosmic rays. His research team took nearly 400 photographs, in places as diverse as New Zealand and Panama, over territory that covered 50,000 miles. News articles described Compton's movements by air and on water and land as he investigated the elusive rays.

After the survey, Compton addressed a meeting of the American Association for the Advancement of Science. He said that his survey and measurements supported the theory that cosmic rays are mostly electric particles. Work done on cosmic rays in later years showed that these charged particles come from outside the Earth's solar system. It also showed that they have colossal energy, some of them traveling at close to the speed of light.

For Compton, who had been studying X rays in his laboratory, the cosmic rays survey was part of what he later called an "atomic quest." Less than 10 years after the survey, he would agree to work with the U.S. government, helping to develop atomic energy and nuclear bombs during the critical war years.

Arthur Holly Compton was born on September 10, 1892, in Wooster, Ohio. His father, Elias, was a Presbyterian minister with a doctoral degree in psychology. He taught at Wooster College and served as dean of that school for 22 years. Compton's mother,

Great Scientists

Otelia Augspurger Compton, was descended from a religious group called Mennonites, a Protestant denomination that believes in pacifism (opposition to war and violence). His parents were involved with foreign missionary work, so Arthur Compton met children from many different countries while he was growing up.

Arthur Compton later recalled how his mother had encouraged his early interest in science. When he was eight years old, he gave her an essay he had written about elephants. He told her that he had read that African elephants have three toes and that Indian elephants have five, but that he believed the opposite was true.

Reading her son's essay, Otelia Compton knew that Arthur was incorrect. Nonetheless, she told him he had done well to study the matter carefully in order to explain his point of view. As an adult, Compton thanked his mother for her understanding, saying, "If you had laughed at me then, it would have finished my urge for research."

His study of elephants was just one expression of Compton's early interest in science. He claimed that he first heard of atomic energy when his father and brother Karl were discussing a newspaper article about the discovery of radium by Marie and Pierre Curie. He was fascinated to learn that radium glowed in the dark and could maintain its warm temperature for thousands of years. Compton found himself thinking, "Where did that heat come from? A continuing flow of energy! Here was one of the wonders of my youthful years."

Although all four Compton children had household chores, they were allowed time to pursue personal interests, which included reading, writing, and sports. Arthur Compton took up astronomy, examining the nighttime sky with a telescope his parents had bought for him in Switzerland. At school, he excelled in mathematics, physics, and other science courses. He built several gliders and wrote articles about aeronautics, three of which were published when he was in high school. When he was 15, he flew in his 30-foot glider above a local golf course.

Like his older brothers, Compton attended Wooster College, taking a job to pay some of his expenses. He had planned to study mechanical engineering, but his brother Karl and several teachers encouraged him to study math and physics. At college, Compton continued to study the solar system, taking pictures of stars and planets with a camera he had attached to his telescope. He worked to improve an astronomical clock that he had built in high school with parts from regular clocks.

Arthur Holly Compton

In 1913, Compton received his bachelor's degree in physics. He also earned a Phi Beta Kappa key along with an athletic letter for football. Again, he followed the example of brother Karl, enrolling in the graduate school of physics at Princeton University. There he was thrilled to hear a lecture by Ernest Rutherford. The British physicist had discovered that an atom, once thought to be the smallest particle of matter, is made up of still smaller parts. The nucleus, he found, was much smaller than the atom itself and contained most of an atom's mass. Scientists discovered it also is the part of the atom that contains the energy that may be exhibited as radioactivity.

As he learned about nuclear physics, Compton decided to do research in this field; "I . . . dreamed of a time when I might work in a laboratory devoted to the study of the energy within the atom. Might it not be that someday we could learn how this could be released for doing the work of man?"

A deeply religious man with Mennonite roots, Compton was distressed about World War I, which raged during his years at Princeton. He had always opposed the use of military force to settle disputes. But later, he wrote about his reluctant acceptance of the idea "that a nation cannot of itself determine to remain at peace." Compton said, "I had seen war come, not because our nation wanted it but because we had been forced by powers bent on military conquest. . . ."

Compton received his Ph.D. in 1916. In the meantime, he had developed and patented a gyroscopic device that could be used to help an airplane maintain its balance. He married Betty Charity McCloskey, a native of New Waterford, Ohio. They moved to Minnesota, where Compton taught physics at the University of Minnesota. To aid the war effort, Compton also worked with the U.S. Army Signal Corps to improve airplane instruments.

After leaving the university, Compton took a job in private industry, as a research engineer at Westinghouse Electric and Manufacturing Company. He worked on electrical lamps for industrial use. After two years, he missed academic life and qualified for a research fellowship at Cavendish Laboratory in Cambridge, England. There he studied atomic physics with such prominent physicists as J. J. Thomson, who had been the first person to identify and weigh an electron, a negatively charged subatomic particle, and Ernest Rutherford, whom he had met at Princeton. The Comptons toured Europe, witnessing the damage left by World War I.

In 1920, Compton returned to the United States, where he became head of the department of physics at Washington University in St. Louis, Missouri. In 1923, he and Betty moved again, to Chicago, where Compton was to head the famous physics department at the University of Chicago. There he was able to teach in the morning and conduct research during the afternoon. His well-equipped office contained a cosmic-ray counter, clicking in one corner of the room.

During the early 1920s, Arthur Compton spent most of his time studying X rays. Compton investigated the photoelectric effect, which stated that different types of radiant energy—for example, X rays, radio waves, and light waves—behave both like particles and like waves. One series of experiments showed that after X rays collide with matter, their wavelength increases.

Compton found that when X rays collide with electrons, they pass some of their own energy to the electron. The energy decrease of the X ray thus causes an increase in its wavelength as the X ray continues on its path. When the paths of the colliding particles are photographed, it shows that radiant energy is a form of matter. This discovery became known as the Compton Effect. It was an important finding that gave added support to Einstein's theory that light is composed of particles.

In addition, Compton used X rays to measure the interior of an atom. For his X-ray work, he used extremely delicate instruments, one of which was said to measure "one ten-millionth of the energy of a mosquito climbing an inch of screen."

In 1927, Arthur Compton was awarded the Nobel Prize in physics (also given that year to C. T. R. Wilson) for his research in "the behavior of X-rays and electrons." He was honored with the Rumford Gold Medal, given by the American Academy of Arts and Sciences. Interviewed in Ohio, the Compton family said that they were proud of Arthur, his mother adding that she hoped the Nobel Prize would not "turn his head."

When Arthur Compton set out on his three-year survey, he was eager to find out how the penetrating rays, which made for a continual cosmic "rain" on Earth, got into the atmosphere.

As a result of Compton's survey and the work of many other scientists, information has accumulated about cosmic rays since the 1930s. Today, scientists divide cosmic rays into two basic groups. the primary rays consist chiefly of protons (hydrogen nuclei, positively charged subatomic particles) and alpha particles (helium nuclei, each one consisting of two protons and two

Compton gets ready to launch a balloon with a small cosmic radiation detector attached to it.
(Courtesy of Washington University in St. Louis Photographic Service)

neutrons), some electrons, and some nuclei of heavier elements. Although some primary rays may come from the sun, most probably travel to Earth from exploding stars located farther off in space. Secondary rays originate when primary rays enter the Earth's atmosphere and then collide with oxygen and nitrogen. Subatomic particles—including electrons, positrons, mesons, and neutrinos—result, and some secondary rays continue to collide, producing even more secondary rays. Secondary ray studies were particularly important during the 1930s. Scientists did not yet have particle accelerators or other kinds of equipment that would later prove so useful in studying the atomic nucleus. By using secondary rays, scientists could discover new elementary particles of the atom.

After his global survey, Compton returned home to Chicago where he and Betty were rearing two sons, Arthur and John. Betty Compton and Arthur Jr., then a young teenager, had gone on the survey, and Compton frequently praised their work on the trip. Compton resumed his position at the University of Chicago and enjoyed his hobbies—tennis, swimming, and playing the mandolin. He continued to teach at the Community Church Sunday school. In 1938 he assumed an important nonscientific post as Protestant co-chairman of the National Conference of Christians and Jews.

As the 1930s ended, Europe was again in the midst of an expanding war, begun by the German dictator Adolf Hitler. In 1939, President Franklin Roosevelt received a letter signed by Albert Einstein and written primarily by the Hungarian-born physicist Leo Szilard, warning that Nazi Germany was working to make atomic weapons. Roosevelt asked some well-known scientists to pursue this subject and to suggest what might be done in the United States. In 1941, Arthur Compton was asked to play a key role in this research and development.

Like many scientists in America, Compton knew about the research in nuclear fission, or the splitting of atomic nuclei, that had been done in Germany. James B. Conant, dean of Harvard University, was part of the steering committee for the U.S. project. He asked Compton to "get together the people who can judge the merits of this atomic bomb proposal, study it, and give us a report on its feasibility."

Compton discussed the question with prominent scientists, including his friend Ernest O. Lawrence, a physicist at the University of California, and his brother Karl, now president of the Massachusetts Institute of Technology (MIT). Wanting to answer a question about uranium fission, Compton asked a physics professor at the University of Chicago, "To whom should I go to get the most reliable calculations on the critical size needed to set up a chain reaction in U-235?" Samuel Allison replied, "No one can answer that question as well as Enrico Fermi."

Fermi was an Italian-born, Nobel Prize–winning physicist who had fled Fascist Italy with his family and was teaching at Columbia University. He had conducted many experiments with radiation during the 1930s. After meeting with Fermi and others,

Compton reported that he thought nuclear bombs could indeed be developed. By then, Compton says, it seemed clear that America would soon be drawn into the war. Said Compton, "We in the United States then saw for the first time that exploration of the possibility of atomic bombs was a military necessity for the safety of the nation. It was then that American scientists began to throw themselves into this exploration with everything they had."

After President Roosevelt ordered that the bomb project (Manhattan Project) be set up without delay, Compton organized what was called the S-1 Committee, under the Office of Scientific Research and Development. Its goal was to create a nuclear chain reaction.

On December 7, 1941, a day after the president's directive, the Japanese bombed Pearl Harbor. Compton's dream of finding a way to harness the power of the atom was coming true, although not under the conditions he had envisioned as a young man. The politics of war now implied that the first use of atomic power would be for weapons of destruction.

Events moved quickly, as the armed forces became involved in the project. Sites for atomic research and the actual building of the bomb were found at Oak Ridge, Tennessee, the Argonne Laboratory near Chicago, and Los Alamos in New Mexico. For the next three years, 1942–45, Compton directed the part of the bomb-building project code-named the Metallurgical Laboratory. He gathered the members of this project in Chicago, including the group led by Enrico Fermi and Leo Szilard, which had been working on small atomic piles in New York City.

On December 2, 1942, a month before the deadline Compton had set for this phase of the research, the S-1 group gathered to try the experiment. The pile devised by Fermi and Compton was the world's first atomic reactor. It was a high cubical pile of graphite bricks and uranium, located in the most spacious and secure area they could find at the University of Chicago campus: the squash court located below Stagg Field Stadium.

Compton was among the dozen scientists who watched the pile from the balcony where the instruments and controls were positioned. The "suicide squad," the nickname for a group of men armed with equipment that could dampen a fire on the pile, was ready. Another group of men stood 100 feet away behind concrete walls. They were equipped with remote control instruments capable of setting off an electrical mechanism that would put safety rods in place if the reaction went out of control.

During that afternoon, at Fermi's direction, the control rods inside the pile were pulled out. Compton watched, knowing that the chain reaction should now occur. He later wrote that

[the Geiger] counters registering the rays from the pile began to click faster and faster until the sound became a rattle. . . . Finally after many minutes the meters showed a reading that meant that the radiation reaching the balcony was beginning to be dangerous. "Throw in the safety rods," came Fermi's order. They went in with a clatter. . . . The rattle of the counters died down to an occasional click. I imagine that I can still hear the sigh of relief from the suicide squad. Eugene Wigner produced a bottle of Italian wine and gave it to Fermi. A little cheer went up.

The test had succeeded. It was, said Compton, "a new age . . . the vast reserves of energy held in the nucleus of the atom were at the disposal of man."

After the chain reaction was completed, Arthur Compton called James Conant at Harvard University with the carefully coded message that has since become part of scientific history: "Jim, you'll be happy to know that the Italian navigator has just landed in the new world."

Conant asked, "Is that so, were the natives friendly?"

And Compton replied, "Everyone landed safe and happy."

In December 1943, Compton moved to Oak Ridge, Tennessee, with his wife and 15-year-old son, John. He supervised some of the work at the plant there, designed to produce needed amounts of plutonium. Another important nuclear power plant was set up at Hanford, Washington. These factories processed plutonium and uranium, a slow and laborious task.

It was not until the summer of 1945 that enough of these fissionable materials had been produced so that the first bombs could be made at the Los Alamos, New Mexico site. During the intervening years, Compton had criss-crossed the country, going from Chicago to Los Alamos to Hanford and various other research centers. Of the work at Los Alamos, he said,

Never, I suppose, has there been gathered together in one place for so long a period of time so large a group of competent men of science. Ideas originated and developed with startling speed. Equipment that ordinarily requires years for building was here constructed in months.

Arthur Holly Compton

Arthur Compton was not among those who witnessed the explosion of the first nuclear bomb, the plutonium Fat Man, on July 16, 1945. Although Robert Oppenheimer, scientific director of Los Alamos, had told him in a coded telegram about the upcoming test, Compton feared that his departure would make people suspicious: "It was well known in certain circles of the Chicago Metallurgical Laboratory that our shops were working day and night fabricating instruments and other structures that were to become part of the bombs. I could not absent myself at that time without giving rise to questions."

The morning of the test, Compton received another coded message from Oppenheimer telling him that "we caught a very big fish." Compton knew what he meant.

As he had played a key role in developing the bomb, now Compton was asked to be part of a select panel of scientists and government officials who groped with the military and ethical problems of its use. By this time, Germany had surrendered. Japan was still at war and refused to surrender.

Compton had wondered about the possibility of using the bomb in a demonstration or perhaps on an unpopulated area of Japan. Yet the committee worried that if it were forewarned, Japan might shoot down the bomber or bring Allied prisoners of war to the area. They also worried about the results of a failed test. They considered the potential loss of lives if the bomb were not used and an invasion of Japan took place instead.

The panel decided that there was no feasible alternative to the military use of the bomb. In the end, they believed that its use would ultimately prevent the great loss of lives that would occur in a prolonged war. Compton had many misgivings about the decision, and said:

> I knew all too well the destruction and human agony the bombs would cause. I knew the danger they held in the hands of some future tyrant. These facts I had been living with for four years. But I wanted the war to end. I wanted life to become normal again. I saw a chance for an enduring peace that would be demanded by the very destructiveness of these weapons. . . . If . . . it would result in the shortening of the war and the saving of lives—if it would mean bringing us closer to the time when war would be abandoned as a means for settling international disputes—here must be our hope and our basis for courage.

Compton was in Chicago when he heard about the bombing of Hiroshima, Japan, on August 6, 1945. The city was destroyed and 100,000 people, one-third of the population, died, while almost all the others were injured in some way. He recalls that there was a "tremendous psychological shock" expressed by people, as they tried to comprehend the power of this frightening new weapon. When Japan still did not surrender, President Harry Truman authorized the dropping of a second bomb, on Nagasaki, Japan, three days later. "Again a blinding flash followed by a pillar of fire and cloud," said Compton. After that attack, Japan surrendered, ending the war.

Arthur Compton went back to Washington University, this time as chancellor. He also taught natural history from the years 1953 to 1961. Like some of the other scientists who had worked on the project to build the bomb, Compton also worked to promote the peacetime uses of atomic energy. He helped to establish the School of Nuclear Science and Engineering at Argonne National Laboratory near Chicago. Students from numerous countries have come to Argonne to learn about atomic energy. Compton advocated a program to give developing nations technical information they needed to develop their own nuclear power plants.

He remained interested in the use of nuclear reactors, especially when they enabled scientists to use new methods for diagnosing and treating diseases, and he studied the use of radioactive isotopes (new forms of elements) in treating cancer.

Believing that with such massive weapons now available in the world, "brotherhood is a condition of our survival," Compton spent the rest of his life involved in efforts to unite people of different nations. He said, "In the postwar world, our contacts must be world contacts."

Compton served as a U.S. delegate to various United Nations conferences in 1946 and 1947. Also during 1947, he participated in the International Emergency Conference to Combat Anti-Semitism, held in Seelisberg, Switzerland. He worked on projects to help Jewish people who had been "displaced" by the Nazi persecution of the 1930s and 1940s. Compton believed that a fight against prejudice was essential in preventing future wars.

In 1949, Compton traveled to India, as chairman of another American delegation for world relief. The next year, he joined 200 Protestant, Roman Catholic, and Jewish leaders from 15 Western European countries in forming an organization called World Brotherhood. As general chairman, Compton helped to state the

Compton enjoyed working with young people, both as a teacher and through the organization World Brotherhood.
(Courtesy of Washington University in St. Louis Photographic Service)

goals of World Brotherhood: to achieve human rights—justice, understanding, and cooperation among nations. Toward these goals, Compton organized meetings at which people, especially young people, could meet others of different races, religions, and nationalities. Such meetings were held in dozens of different countries during the next decade.

While promoting World Brotherhood, Arthur Compton continued to serve as chancellor of Washington University. He resigned, however, in 1952 so that he could do more writing, including the book *Atomic Quest*. He also wanted to spend more time studying, as he put it, "science and its relation to human affairs." Serving as chairman of World Brotherhood's Commission on Scientific Research, Compton examined issues dealing with the social changes that accompany changing scientific and technical developments.

On March 15, 1962, after a remarkable career in science and public life, Arthur Compton died in St. Louis. His religious view of life had once led him to say, "Science is the glimpse of God's purpose in nature and the very existence of the amazing world of the atom and radiation points to a purposeful creation, to the idea that there is a God and an intelligent purpose back of everything."

As director of the Metallurgical Project, Compton had been one of the first people to recognize the hazards to workers that were exposed to radiation. He is considered to be a pioneer in the field of health physics for his attempts to prevent such hazards. At times, he had delayed work on the assembly line in order to analyze risks and decide what type of protection—masks, shields, monitoring devices, alarm signals, ventilation, and checks of safety equipment—might be needed. He also helped to develop a laundry system that would decontaminate the items used in the plants.

Besides his achievements as a scientist and citizen, Compton was admired for the courtesy that he showed others throughout his lifetime. Writing about this in her book *Atoms in the Family*, Laura Fermi said that Arthur Compton was "a thoughtful and considerate person, who took no step without weighing its effects on others. Perhaps because of this, whenever he expressed an opinion, it was interpreted as an order and accepted without much comment."

Compton's personal traits, along with his scientific ability, had enabled him to perform a unique role during a painful time in world history. He had witnessed the climactic outcome of his atomic quest and gone on to work for world peace and understanding.

Chronology

September 10, 1892	Arthur Holly Compton born in Wooster, Ohio
1908	publishes three articles about aeronautics
1913	graduates with degree in physics from Wooster College
1916	receives Ph.D. in physics from Princeton University
1918–20	Research fellow at the Cavendish Laboratory in Cambridge, England
1920	appointed professor of physics, Washington University, St. Louis, Missouri
1923	becomes head of University of Chicago Ryerson (physics) Laboratory
1927	awarded the Nobel Prize in physics; receives Rumford Gold Medal of the American Academy of Arts and Sciences
1930–33	conducts world-wide survey of cosmic rays
1938	installed as Protestant co-chairman of National Conference of Christians and Jews (1938–48)
1941	appointed head of scientists' group to study feasibility of atomic weapons
1941	appointed by U.S. government to lead research unit to develop a nuclear chain reaction
April 1942	supervises scientists working in lab code-named the Metallurgical Laboratory

December 2, 1942	witnesses successful nuclear chain reaction
1943–45	supervises production of plutonium; directs other scientific work for the Manhattan Project
1945	returns to teaching; appointed chancellor of Washington University (until 1952)
1947–48	appointed U.S. delegate to UN conferences working for post-war relief
1949	helps to establish World Brotherhood
1953–61	appointed professor of natural history at Washington University
1956	publishes *Atomic Quest*
March 15, 1962	dies at age 69

Further Reading

Bolton, Sarah K. *Famous Men of Science*. New York: Crowell, 1960. Profiles of Arthur Compton, as well as his brother Karl, and other famous American scientists.

Compton, Arthur Holly. *Atomic Quest*. New York: Oxford University Press, 1956. Compton's account of his lifelong interest in atomic power and his research and wartime work in this field.

Fermi, Laura. *Atoms in the Family: My Life with Enrico Fermi*. Chicago: University of Chicago Press, 1954. A biography of Enrico Fermi by his wife; her account of the people and events leading to the first nuclear chain reaction and atomic bombs.

———. *The Story of Atomic Energy*. New York: Random House, 1961. History of important scientific work that led to the development of atomic power and its various military and peaceful uses.

Friedlander, Michael W. *Cosmic Rays*. Cambridge, Massachusetts: Harvard University Press, 1989. Describes cosmic ray research up to the present and shows how such research has been used.

Groueff, Stephane. *Manhattan Project*. Boston: Little, Brown, 1967. A thorough account of the people and events that culminated in the development of atomic bombs in 1945. For older readers.

Hethcote, Niels H. de V. *Breakthroughs in Twentieth Century Science: Nobel Prize Winners in Physics 1901–1950*. New York: Henry Schuman, 1953. A closer look at Compton's work with radiation, leading to his Nobel Prize in physics.

Kurtzman, Dan. *Day of the Bomb: Countdown to Hiroshima*. New York: McGraw-Hill, 1986. Traces the scientific and military events that led to the building and use of the first atomic bomb in 1945.

Linus Carl Pauling:
Seeking Molecules and Peace

Linus Pauling in his official Nobel Prize portrait.
(Courtesy of the California Institute of Technology)

*O*ne spring day in 1948, a scientist sat in bed, recovering from a cold and a kidney infection. Although he could not give his scheduled lectures at Oxford University, where he was a visiting professor, Dr. Linus Pauling was hard at work. He was thinking about an important question that had intrigued him for years. How were protein molecules constructed? If scientists solved this problem, they could learn the workings of living tissues—skin, hair, muscle, bone, blood—for all these tissues consist of protein molecules.

For more than 10 years, Pauling had studied proteins in his chemistry laboratory. He knew that protein molecules are long chains composed of a series of 20 different kinds of amino acids, the chemical "building blocks" of protein. The amino acids are joined to each other with chemical linkages called peptide bonds, forming a chain called a polypeptide.

Pauling had worked with Robert B. Corey and others to find the precise form that a polypeptide chain takes in proteins. As was his practice, he made models of molecules out of string, rod-and-ball structures, and soft plastic bubbles in different shapes, sizes and colors. Because of this, students and faculty at the California Institute of Technology, where Pauling was a professor, spoke of his "baby toy lectures," in which the famous chemist used such models to illustrate scientific principles.

That day Pauling did not have his models. He sketched drawings of atoms and chemical bonds on pieces of paper. Folding them different ways, he eventually formed a helix—a three-dimensional shape resembling a spiral. Pauling later said, "I folded the paper to bend one bond at the right angle, what I thought it should be relative to the other, and kept doing this, making a helix, until I could form hydrogen bonds between one turn of the helix and the next run of the helix, and it only took a few hours of doing that to discover the alpha helix."

Pauling had discovered the basic structure of the protein molecule. Although he could not prove he was correct on that day, scientists later found that these vital materials of life—proteins—were indeed spiral, single-helical shapes. This new knowledge enabled scientists to learn more about biological tissues. Pauling and Corey eventually worked out the structure of the molecules that make up muscle, fingernail, hair, horn, silk, bone, tusk, and other tissues. Their helical models met demanding tests for accuracy. They concluded that a helix is the basic shape of protein in life forms, regardless of their kind.

It was not the first time that Linus Pauling had made an important contribution to science, nor would it be the last. He did notable work in studying blood hemoglobin, sickle-cell anemia, anesthesia, psychiatry, and nutrition. Pauling has also made a strong impact on methods of scientific research. Often, he used his reasoning abilities first to guess the structure of a molecule, then to test it. His techniques of intuition and model building have been copied by other scientists. Called by many the "greatest chemist of the 20th century," Pauling has also been a political activist, believing that scientists have a responsibility in this arena, too.

―――――――――

Linus Carl Pauling was born on February 28, 1901, outside of Portland, Oregon. The rural area had been settled by farmers and men who traveled west to build bridges and railroads or to work on cattle drives. Linus was the first child of Herman William Pauling and his wife, Lucy Isabelle Darling. By 1905, the family included two daughters, named Pauline and Frances Lucille.

The Paulings lived in a one-room apartment but had trouble living on Herman's wages as a druggist and part-time salesman. Looking for more opportunities, they moved to nearby Condon, then to Portland, the capital of Oregon.

By the time Linus was nine years old, the people around him were already impressed by his curiosity and intelligence. His sister Lucille once recalled, "Linus was always thinking." Herman Pauling wrote a letter to the *Oregonian*, a local newspaper, asking for suggestions about ways to develop Linus's abilities. That same year, Herman Pauling died at age 32.

Pauling showed an early interest in mathematics, then in natural science. He later said, "When I was around 11 or 12, on my own initiative I made a collection of insects. I'd often get a book from the library and started collecting insects and classifying them, and I had become interested in minerals." At age 13, the future chemist built a small lab in the basement, even though he did not have much money to buy equipment or supplies. His love of science flourished during a general science course he took as a freshman in high school. Pauling later praised Pauline Geballe, who taught the course, as an inspiring and outstanding educator.

By then, his widowed mother was running a rooming house to support the family. Pauling held various jobs before and after school. He delivered milk, operated a motion picture projector in a theater, and worked in shipyards on the Willamette River.

Pauling finished Washington High School in 1917 and wanted to enter college as an engineering student (the path to a science career in those years). Pauling later said that his mother discouraged this idea, pointing out that no other neighborhood young people were going to college and that Linus would earn more money by working full time. But Pauling had made up his mind.

When his mother asked why he insisted upon continuing his education, he recalls saying, "I want to learn, Mama."

The summer of 1917, Pauling held two jobs to earn money. He started classes in October at Oregon Agricultural College in Corvallis (now Oregon State University). Pauling excelled in his engineering, chemistry, and mathematics classes. He tutored some of the other students at no charge and spent about 100 hours each month working at the school's kitchens and chopping wood for dormitories. Pauling later said that he could afford to attend this college because "there was no tuition, and registration fees were only a few dollars, and books weren't very expensive. I had perhaps $20 worth of books my freshman year, all second-hand. . . ."

Sophomore year, Pauling says, he "limped through . . . with no money" and regularly skipped classes to work at the Tillamook shipyard and as a paving plant inspector. Despite a crowded schedule, Pauling took time to study chemical bonding, a subject he had heard about in class. Chemical bonding is the way in which the atoms of various elements join to form molecules of another, different substance. For example, two hydrogen atoms join one atom of oxygen to make water, which has the chemical symbol H_2O (two hydrogen atoms, one oxygen atom). Atoms join together (or are repelled by each other) depending on their valence, that is, their negative or positive electrical charge. The type of charge depends upon how many electrons (negatively charged subatomic particles) an atom has and the way in which these electrons are arranged.

Pauling read a new theory that said electrons could be "shared"—held in common by more than one atom at a time. This would bond or link the atoms. He later said,

I knew a great amount of descriptive chemistry and I could see how the shared pair of electrons could explain what the forces are that hold the atoms together. I could see that the first steps were being taken toward a real, systematic science of structural chemistry. It was then that I developed a strong desire to understand the physical and chemical properties of substances in relation to the atoms and molecules of which they are made up. This interest has largely determined the course of my research for 50 years.

Family problems disrupted Pauling's junior year. His mother became ill with pernicious anemia. Pauling increased his work schedule, sending her his earnings. He taught a sophomore chemistry course at the college, worked in the lab, gave lectures, and graded papers. In his senior year, he taught more chemistry classes, to home economics students, and began dating Ava Helen Miller, who had been a student in one of these classes.

In a metallurgy course, Pauling studied the structure of crystals. These crystallography studies and his study of the chemical bond led to his later efforts to unravel the construction of basic life substances—their molecules and the connections that link them.

Pauling earned enough money to finish college. He made plans to marry Ava Helen and attend graduate school. The California Institute of Technology (Caltech) was then growing into what would become a world-famous scientific center. To meet expenses, Pauling received a fellowship and planned to teach part time. He looked forward to studying chemical bonds and was fortunate to have as a graduate school adviser Roscoe Dickinson, who was known for his work in X-ray crystallography.

In 1912 a German chemist, Max von Laue, had aimed X rays at crystals. He found that the rays were broken up by the crystals into patterns of spots, which showed the positions of different atoms in the crystal molecules. Because various atoms scatter X rays onto photographic plates in a predictable pattern, scientists can use the X rays to figure out the arrangement of atoms that the substance contains. This information helped scientists to discover the structures of molecules, including the distances between atoms and the kinds of angles between chemical bonds.

Together, Pauling and Dickinson studied the structure of inorganic (nonliving) matter, examining minerals with the rough equipment available at that time. Pauling returned to work as a paving plant inspector in 1923, so he could send money home. That year, he and Ava Helen were married.

In 1924 a grant let him conduct full-time research. During graduate school. Pauling juggled research, teaching, classes, and odd jobs. Yet he received his doctorate, with high honors, in 1925. His doctoral paper, or dissertation, was about the atomic structure of crystals. Also that year, he and Ava Helen welcomed their first child, son Linus Jr.

Pauling knew that in Europe, scientists were studying chemical bonds and applying the new ideas of quantum mechanics to chemistry as well as physics. Quantum mechanics is a set of laws that apply to the behavior of atoms and subatomic particles—the nucleus, electrons, and protons (positively charged subatomic particles) that make up an atom. Pauling was one of 35 people who received fellowships from the Guggenheim Foundation in 1925. He arranged to study at the University of Munich.

In Europe, Pauling worked with some world-acclaimed physicists—Arnold Sommerfeld in Munich, Germany, Niels Bohr in Copenhagen, Denmark, Erwin Schrödinger in Zurich, Switzerland, and Sir William Henry Bragg in London, England. These experiences gave Pauling new insights into his research with bond angles and crystal structures.

In 1927, Pauling returned to the United States as assistant professor of chemistry at Caltech. The family moved into a small frame house. Pauling published a widely praised paper, in which he used theories of quantum mechanics to clarify the structure of the carbon atom. Pauling's "resonance theory" was hailed as a great achievement. The theory combined knowledge about chemical bonds (from the field of chemistry) with knowledge about electrons (from the field of physics). Pauling said that there are inner vibrations (resonances) of atoms that create forces that bind molecules together. He described atoms as being linked together in such a way as to form definite patterns. Pauling claimed that the molecules formed as a result of such patterns have a certain geometrical shape that can be predicted.

Pauling's theory of resonance helped scientists to learn more about the geometry of molecules, or structural chemistry. As a result, scientists have learned much about the properties (traits) of matter. One practical outcome of this research is that scientists can often predict the behaviors of new substances they are planning to make in their laboratories. This research, along with Pauling's later studies of chemical bonds, aided the development of synthetic drugs, as well as plastics and fibers.

As the 1920s ended, Pauling's interest shifted to organic, or living, matter. This interest in life sciences was partly inspired by geneticist Thomas Hunt Morgan, who arrived at Caltech in 1929. According to Pauling, Morgan's work helped him to "become familiar with biological problems" and to look at biological questions in light of his understanding of molecular chemistry. Said Pauling, "I had become interested enough in genetics to present a seminar describing a theory of the crossing-over of chromosomes that I had developed."

During those years, the science of protein chemistry was young. In 1934, Pauling began to study an organic molecule: hemoglobin, a large protein molecule found in blood that gives blood its red color. Hemoglobin picks up oxygen in the lungs, then carries it to other areas as blood circulates throughout the body. After working with hemoglobin, Pauling decided to study protein molecules by starting at the most basic point: the atomic structure of the amino acids that make up proteins.

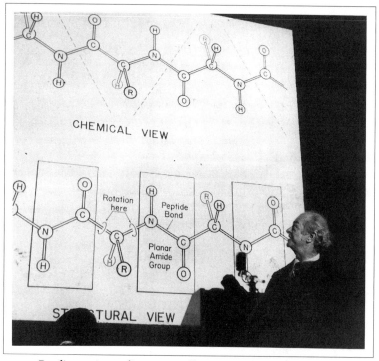

Pauling using a diagram to illustrate a chemistry lecture.
(Courtesy of the California Institute of Technology)

In 1937, he was appointed director of the Caltech laboratory. He continued to study chemical bonds and in 1939 published a book, *The Nature of the Chemical Bond and the Structure of Molecules and Crystals*. It became one of the most significant scientific textbooks of the 20th century. Pauling's growing reputation attracted students and researchers to the chemistry department at Caltech.

Pauling showed skill in areas besides science. At Caltech, Albert Einstein once attended a conference at which Pauling presented a paper in German. Einstein asked how he had become so fluent in the language. Pauling replied that he had spent a year studying in Germany. According to Professor W. K. Ferrier, as quoted by Pauling's biographer Anthony Serafini, Einstein said that Pauling had learned to speak better German in one year than he, Einstein, had learned to speak English in two years.

Pauling's work was interrupted in the fall of 1940. He became ill with Bright's disease, a serious kidney ailment that can be fatal. Pauling's doctor advised a low protein diet to rest the kidneys and extra vitamin C. This experience may have influenced Pauling's later interest in nutrition and vitamin C treatments.

After his recovery, Pauling returned to work. Major political events were taking place in the world. As World War II ravaged more countries, military research was stressed at Caltech and other scientific centers. The Caltech faculty issued a memorandum that said "we have volunteered [our] personal services to assist the government in the present world emergency to the utmost of [our] abilities." Pauling opposed fascism and the fascist governments in Germany and Italy and offered to do research for the U.S. government. To aid the military, he worked with meters used to measure the oxygen pressure in submarines, explosives and liquid propellants for rockets, and chemicals to improve gunpowder.

He also continued to study living cells. In 1942, with Dr. Don Campbell and Dr. David Pressman, Pauling showed that the production of antibodies—protein substances in the blood that fight disease—stems from changes in the shape of serum globulins, a type of protein molecule in the blood. They found that antibodies fight antigens—disease-causing substances in the blood—by fastening themselves to the surfaces of these attacking agents in order to deactivate them. Pauling compared this to the way a key fits into a lock: the antibody fits the particular virus or germ that it was shaped to fit, not others. This team of scientists changed the shape of sample serum globulins to make antibodies in test tubes.

After the United States entered the war, the Pauling family had a new worry. Linus Jr. had joined the air corps. Some of Pauling's students at Caltech were also serving in the military. In 1943, the Paulings found themselves involved in a political controversy. A gardener who worked at their California home was an American of Japanese descent. After the bombing of Pearl Harbor in December 1941, the Paulings got threatening mail and phone calls. A red-painted message appeared on their garage door: "Americans die, but we love japs." Says Pauling, "We received some threats through the mail, directed at my wife and children, and for two weeks the sheriff kept a twenty-four hour guard around our house, while I was making a trip to Washington, D.C." The gardener later left to serve in the U.S. Army. This experience increased Linus Pauling's interest in politics. He and Ava Helen spoke out against the internment of Japanese-Americans into camps during the war.

In 1945, Pauling and Campbell led a team that was able to make a substitute for blood plasma from gelatin. This substitute, called oxpolygelatin, was then used successfully in blood transfusions. It is cheaper and easier to get than plasma taken from human blood, which depends upon an adequate supply of blood donors.

After the war, Linus Jr. returned safely from the army and attended Pomona College. The Paulings' son Peter was studying physics and biology. Linda, age 15, enjoyed the arts, as well as reading. Crellin, the youngest, was 10. Pauling had become concerned about nuclear weapons after the bombing of Japan. As an expert on chemical explosives, he was sometimes asked to lecture on nuclear and other military weapons. Pauling became alarmed about the destructive potential of nuclear weapons, and thought that people around the world should know the risks and ask their governments not to use these weapons.

In 1946 in California, Pauling and Robert Oppenheimer, the scientist who had headed the project that developed the first atomic bombs, organized a meeting to form the Pasadena Federation of Atomic Scientists; a similar federation had been founded in Chicago. Both groups planned to spread knowledge about the dangers of atomic energy. Pauling also joined the Emergency Committee of Atomic Scientists (known as the Einstein Committee) chaired by Albert Einstein, which aimed to educate people about atomic weapons. By this time, the Soviet Union also had an atomic bomb. Pauling was concerned about the development of the hydrogen bomb and spoke against it from 1947 through 1950. The hydrogen bomb was a fusion bomb, more destructive than the fission-types that were built during World War II.

Although Pauling had not spent much time on political issues, Ava Helen Pauling had been actively involved in such causes for years. She belonged to organizations that worked for peace and civil liberties. Both Linus and Ava Helen Pauling had supported President Franklin D. Roosevelt and his policies during the Great Depression.

Linus Carl Pauling

In 1947, Pauling received an important honor—the Presidential Medal of Merit—for his contributions to science and humanity. President Harry S Truman bestowed the award, commenting on Pauling's work on crystal structures, his insights into the nature of chemical bonding, and his efforts toward world peace.

Then, in 1948, Pauling made his pivotal discovery of the alpha helix form of proteins, while twisting pieces of paper. He led the way for scientists to find out how various atoms in protein are joined together, in what order, and at what intervals. This was no easy task because proteins are complex substances. Most chemical compounds have only a few hundred atoms, but protein molecules can contain thousands, even millions, of atoms. Thousands of different proteins operate inside the human body.

Pauling, Corey, and their assistants applied their knowledge of chemical bonds to the problem. They studied the structure of individual amino acids and polypeptides and considered what linkages were most likely to occur. Pauling used the X ray diffraction techniques that he had learned in earlier years, but now he aimed X rays at crystallized molecules of organic compounds to see how the rays were scattered. This helped him to guess the positions of the atoms within the substances.

By 1953, the researchers knew the structure of collagen, muscle, nail, hair, and other proteins. Biologists had valuable information with which to study proteins such as those that made up cancer cells. Pauling's research and methods also helped James Watson and Francis Crick to deduce the structure of the DNA molecule a few years later.

In the late 1940s, Pauling had begun to study sickle-cell anemia. Found among people of African descent, sickle-cell anemia involves changed blood cells. The red blood cells of those with the disease have a deformity that shows up as a sickled shape, but only when the blood has been taken from veins. Red blood cells in the arterial circulation have the normal disclike shape. Disc-shaped cells pass through blood vessels comfortably, but the stiffer, sickled cells may form clumps. They have trouble passing through vessels. Thus, they cannot carry as much oxygen to body cells or remove the waste product of carbon dioxide as effectively. Afflicted people may suffer from shortness of breath, fever, joint pain, and strokes. Often, they die in childhood.

Pauling thought that sickle-cell disease stemmed from an abnormal hemoglobin molecule—one with a defect in its atomic structure. He believed that this abnormality occurred because of a gene mutation that was inherited. To check his theories, Pauling got blood from sickle-cell patients, then separated abnormal cells from others. His research showed that the red pigment (heme) was the same in both sickle and normal cells. But the protein globin in the sickle cells was different. It did not respond the same way under an electrical field. Sickle-cell globin has a stronger positive charge than normal. Chemical reactions depend upon valence—the positive or negative charge—so the difference in the sickle-cell molecule caused it to react differently with oxygen and carbon dioxide.

Pauling said that sickle-cell anemia comes from a mutation in the gene that is responsible for producing hemoglobin. Like all proteins, hemoglobin is made up of amino acids. But the defective gene follows the wrong atomic pattern, substituting the amino acid valine where glutamic acid normally goes. This gives the molecule its abnormal (positive) electrical charge, enabling it to carry hemoglobin and carbon dioxide. Although no cure for the disease is yet known, Pauling's 1949 research into the cause has led to progress in diagnosis and treatment. People may also take a test to see if they are carrying the gene that causes sickle-cell anemia.

At the same time that he was making advances in his lab, Pauling increased his political activities. During a January 1950 meeting, he and Albert Einstein talked about ethics and politics, expressing concern about the threat of nuclear war. In a letter to Leo Szilard, another scientist who shared these concerns, Pauling wrote, ". . . the question of peace or war has now become so important as to overshadow all other questions—it is of a far greater order of magnitude than anything else."

Pauling's increased political activities took some time away from his research. He undertook an effort to get thousands of other scientists to sign petitions banning nuclear testing. As a result of his activism, Pauling was asked to testify before a congressional investigating committee in California in 1950. He released a press statement that said, in part, "My own political views are well known. I am not a Communist. I have never been involved with the Communist Party. I am a Rooseveltian Democrat. I believe that it is of the greatest importance that citizens take political action, in order that our Nation not deteriorate."

The McCarthy era, as it came to be known, had begun. In California, members of the Communist party, among other politically active people, were targeted for investigation. Pauling found these investigations distasteful. He objected to the loyalty oaths that state employees and others were asked to take, saying that people should not be required to identify their political beliefs in front of committees of other people. He refused to do so, as a matter of principle.

Pauling had planned to attend a meeting in England to discuss his theories about protein structure, but the U.S. government denied him a passport. Pauling wrote to President Dwight Eisenhower, saying, "I am a loyal citizen of the United States. I have never been guilty of any unpatriotic or criminal act. . . ." Still unable to get a passport, he wrote to Secretary of State Dean Acheson, contending that preventing scientists from attending meetings would hurt America's reputation abroad. In 1952, other scientists, including Enrico Fermi, Harold Urey, and Edward Teller, wrote to Acheson in support of Pauling's efforts to get a passport.

Science historians have said that a trip to England at that time might have enabled Pauling to figure out the DNA molecule. At labs in England, Rosalind Franklin and Maurice Wilkins had taken X-ray photos of crystallized DNA. Pauling would probably have asked to see them. Biographer Anthony Serafini says, "Had he been able to travel to England in 1952, he might well have beaten Watson and Crick in the legendary and much publicized race to unravel the structure of the DNA molecule."

Unable to travel, Pauling held a conference in Pasadena for British scientists. At this 1953 conference, some of the scientists who had disputed his protein theories decided Pauling might be correct after all. That same year, Pauling's book *No More War!* was published. Again Pauling missed international conferences because he was denied a passport. (A few years later, Robert Oppenheimer was also in this situation, having been declared a "security risk" by the U.S. Atomic Energy Commission in June 1959. At a graduation speech at Reed College in Oregon that year, Pauling defended Oppenheimer, saying that during these troubling times, people were "not thinking clearly.")

In the midst of these problems, Pauling heard that he had won the 1954 Nobel Prize in chemistry for his work in describing the general shape and organization of proteins. The telephone call notifying him about the award came while he was lecturing about hemoglobin at Cornell University, November 3, 1954. Yet Pauling still had no passport with which to travel to the December ceremony in Sweden. Once again, he completed a passport application. Prestigious scientists spoke on his behalf. Just two weeks before the ceremony, a passport was finally issued to him.

Returning to Caltech, Pauling continued to work for peace. In 1957, he urged scientists to sign a petition asking for a nuclear test ban treaty. Pauling declared, "I believe that no human being should be sacrificed . . . to the project of perfecting nuclear weapons that could kill hundreds of millions of human beings, could devastate this beautiful world in which we live." The petition, called the "Pauling Appeal," was signed by 10,000 scientists from different countries. On the other side of this debate were scientists such as Hungarian-born Edward Teller (called Father of the H-Bomb) who said that the best route to peace was through nuclear superiority.

In 1961, a Senate subcommittee asked Pauling to name volunteers who had helped to circulate the Pauling Appeal. He refused. No charges were filed against him. The press reported his activities. Some journalists praised him; others were critical. Some people labeled Pauling overly idealistic.

Why did Pauling subject himself to criticism and other problems to fight for social causes? He has said that his activism came "out of a sense of duty, conscience, not because I like doing it—also because my wife felt I was doing the right thing." He has also said, "I have contended that scientists . . . have the responsibilities of ordinary citizens, but then they also have a responsibility because of their understanding of science, and of those problems of society in which science is involved closely, to help their fellow citizens to understand, by explaining to them what their own understanding of these problems is."

Political activities did not keep Pauling from doing vital research. After he received the 1953 Nobel Prize, Pauling began to look for possible chemical bases for mental illness. He studied brain chemistry, the protein cells of the brain being among the most complex of all living matter. Among other things, Pauling concluded that certain nutritional elements, such as niacin (vitamin B_3), are needed for the brain to work properly.

In 1963, Pauling won a second Nobel Prize—this time for peace—becoming one of only a few people ever to be thus honored twice and the only person to win the prize twice on his own. He commented, "For many years it has not been respectable to work for peace. Perhaps the Norwegian Nobel Prize Committee's action will help to make it respectable." That year, Pauling also left Caltech, where he had received his doctorate and taught for 36

Pauling beside one of the classroom models he often used to show molecular structure—for his so-called baby toy lectures.
(Courtesy of the California Institute of Technology)

years. He spent the next three years at the Center for the Study of Democratic Institutions in Santa Barbara, California. There, he did no lab work but explored theoretical features of scientific problems.

Pauling moved again in 1967. At age 66 he still chose to teach, this time at the San Diego campus of the University of California, where he continued to study the links between nutrition and mental problems. In 1969, he became professor emeritus at Stanford University at Palo Alto, California. He built a new laboratory there, which continues to be supported with research grants.

Pauling was again the focus of controversy in the 1970s when he wrote *Vitamin C and the Common Cold*. He proposed that large doses of vitamin C might prevent and/or treat colds. Some medical doctors said that Pauling did not have the credentials to draw medical conclusions. Many health care professionals also rejected his findings regarding nutrition and mental illness. But in recent years, research has shown that certain vitamins are needed to produce the chemicals that form important components of the nervous system. Research in this area continues.

In 1972, Pauling received the first Dr. Martin Luther King Medical Achievement Award for his work on sickle-cell anemia. His name had often been suggested for the highest U.S. science award, the National Medal of Science, but was rejected, evidently because of Pauling's political activities, including protesting the war in Vietnam. President Gerald Ford, however, authorized him to receive this honor in 1975. Pauling's award citation noted the "extraordinary power and scope of his imagination which has led to basic contributions in such diverse fields as structural chemistry and the nature of genetic diseases. . . ."

Pauling celebrated his 75th birthday in 1976 at a festive party given at Caltech in his honor. He was pleased that the Linus Pauling Institute had raised enough money to move into a building near the Stanford Linear Accelerator Center in Menlo Park, California. He continued to study vitamin C and other subjects.

Pauling continued to work at the institute, studying cancer, viruses and AIDS (acquired immune deficiency syndrome). He wrote papers about superconductivity, applying chemical bond theories to this process. Well-known physicist Professor P. W. Anderson of Princeton University used Pauling's resonating valence bond approach in his own studies of superconductivity. Anderson credited Pauling's contribution in articles he wrote on this subject.

In 1971, Graham Chedd, a science writer for *New Scientist*, called Pauling, "arguably the greatest scientist alive today." During his life, Pauling greatly advanced many older fields of science and aided the development of new ones. He published more than 500 scientific papers. He was also a distinguished teacher, helping to train new generations of scientists. James D. Watson attended a Pauling lecture in Switzerland and later wrote, "There was no one like Linus in all the world. The combination of his prodigious mind and his infectious grin was unbeatable."

Pauling was not afraid to speak out, either about science or politics. He opposed nuclear weapons and worked for peace when such actions were unpopular. He proposed controversial scientific theories about such subjects as vitamin C. When

Pauling's ideas have not proven to be correct, they have still provoked productive discussions and new research.

Scientist-author Isaac Asimov called Pauling ". . . a first-class genius . . . a brave man who struggled for peace and against nuclear weapons even during the McCarthy era when so many worthy men were frightened and browbeaten into silence . . . he is a gentleman in the highest sense of the word."

Linus Pauling died in 1994 at the age of 93.

Chronology

February 28, 1901	Linus Carl Pauling born near Portland, Oregon
1922	receives B.S. in chemical engineering from Oregon Agricultural College
1925	receives Ph.D. in physical chemistry from Caltech
1927	appointed assistant professor of chemistry at Caltech
1931	appointed full professor of chemistry at Caltech
1934	begins studying hemoglobin
1939	publishes The Nature of the Chemical Bond
1941	receives the Nichols Medal
1945	helps to develop oxpolygelatin
1946	receives Willard Gibbs Medal; begins speaking out against nuclear weapons and the hydrogen bomb; joins Robert Oppenheimer in starting the Pasadena Federation of Atomic Scientists
1947	receives Royal Society of London Davy Medal and the Presidential Medal of Merit
1948	discovers the alpha helix structure of the protein molecule
1954	awarded the Nobel Prize in chemistry
1957	sponsors and collects signatures for the "Pauling Appeal"
1958	publishes *No More War!*

1961	investigated by Senate subcommittee; refuses to identify people who circulated the Pauling Appeal
1963	awarded the Nobel Peace Prize; leaves Caltech to work at the Center for the Study of Democratic Institutions
1967	begins teaching and research at University of California
1969	appointed professor emeritus of chemistry at Stanford University; studies vitamin C and its relation to the common cold
1972	receives first Dr. Martin Luther King Medical Achievement Award for work on sickle-cell anemia
1975	receives National Medal of Science award from President Gerald Ford
1976–1994	continues research on such subjects as cancer, viruses, and superconductivity at the Linus Pauling Institute laboratory in Menlo Park, California
1994	Linus Pauling dies

Further Reading

Farber, Eduard. *Nobel Prize Winners in Chemistry. 1901–1961.* New York: Abelard Schumann, Inc., 1963. Description of Pauling's work with chemical bonding and resonance theory, for which he was awarded the 1954 Nobel Prize in chemistry.

Fry, William F., Jr. "What's New With You, Linus Pauling?" *The Humanist* (Nov.-Dec., 1974), 17. An interview in which Pauling discusses his scientific work and social issues.

Goodell, Rae. *The Visible Scientists*. New York: Harper and Row, 1983. A profile of Pauling, among other well-known scientists; essays describing the impact that Pauling and other famous 20th-century scientists have had on society and public opinion.

Gray, Tony. *Champions of Peace: The Story of Alfred Nobel, The Peace Prize and the Laureates*. New York: Paddington Press, Inc., 1976. A profile of Pauling, focusing on his political and pacifist activities.

Judson, Horace. *The Eighth Day of Creation*. New York: Simon and Schuster, 1979. A comprehensive account of the development of genetics and molecular biology, including DNA research, with extensive footnotes; describes Pauling's work in biology and protein structure. For more advanced students.

Olby, Robert. *The Path to the Double Helix*. Seattle, Washington: University of Washington Press, 1974. A history of the events leading up to the discovery of the structure of the DNA molecule showing contributions of Pauling's theories and models.

Pauling, Linus. *No More War!* New York: Dodd, Mead, 1958. The Nobel laureate speaks out about world peace and the threat of nuclear weapons.

———— and Ewan Cameron. *Cancer and Vitamin C*. New York: Warner Books, 1979. Pauling and fellow researchers discuss their controversial theories about the use of vitamin C to prevent and cure disease.

Serafini, Anthony. *Linus Pauling: A Man and His Science*. New York: Paragon House, 1989. A recent, detailed biography of Pauling with an extensive source list. For older readers.

White, Florence Meiman. *Linus Pauling: Scientist and Crusader*. New York: Walker, 1980. A biography of Pauling, describing his scientific achievements and his political activism; written for young people.

Enrico Fermi:
Unleashing Atomic Power

Enrico Fermi.
(Courtesy of Los Alamos National Laboratory)

*T*he laboratory where about 20 excited people were gathered on the morning of December 2, 1942, was far from ordinary. For one thing, this was top secret research for the United States government. The laboratory had been set up in a squash court located in the basement of Stagg Field Stadium at the University of Chicago. By afternoon, the assembled group would witness one of the most dramatic events in scientific history: the first controlled nuclear chain reaction.

The man directing the experiment was the Italian-American physicist Dr. Enrico Fermi. The stocky, dark-haired scientist stood beside a control panel on a balcony 10 feet above the court floor. Below him stood a pile that seemed to be built of black bricks, stacked nearly 26 feet high. The group waited expectantly as the experiment began. Much was at stake: The U.S. government had spent more than $300,000,000 on secret research projects tied to the work being done by Fermi's team in Chicago.

All the secrecy and expense were because the world was at war. In 1939, several prominent American scientists had realized that an atomic bomb could be made—and that the enemy, Nazi Germany, might make it first. Enrico Fermi was one of the world's leading physicists and one of the few who was highly skilled in both theoretical and experimental physics. He was asked to play a key role in the development of atomic energy, that of producing a controlled and self-sustaining nuclear chain reaction. For this task, he devised a stack of graphite bricks containing uranium, called an atomic pile. Fermi's work with the splitting of atoms proved that people could both release and control nuclear energy. Since 1942, nuclear power had been developed for peacetime energy and for wartime weapons. A prediction Albert Einstein made in 1939 had come true: For the first time, people would use "energy that does not come from the sun."

Enrico Fermi was born on September 29, 1901, in Rome, Italy. He was the youngest of three children born to Alberto and Ida de Gattis Fermi. His sister, Maria, had been born in 1899, followed by brother Giulio in 1900. Alberto Fermi worked as an administrator for the railroad, and Ida was a teacher in the elementary schools. The family lived in a modest apartment near the railroad station.

In his early school years, Enrico excelled in mathematics and science, interests he shared with his brother Giulio. The two boys were also best friends who spent hours together playing, reading, and designing and building mechanical things, such as electric motors. During the winter of 1915, Giulio developed a severe throat abscess. He was admitted to the hospital and died during surgery.

The Fermis were grief-stricken. In a biography that Laura Capon Fermi later wrote about her famous husband, she said that he "kept his grief to himself . . . There was one thing that Enrico could do alone to fill the melancholy hours: study. And study he did, following an avid interest in science."

At school, his teachers noticed Fermi's energy and ability to remember the contents of a book after reading it only once. In his early teens, Fermi admired Galileo and Albert Einstein. He was eager to learn more but had little spending money for books. So Fermi walked two miles to the open market held every Wednesday in Rome to buy used books. Amid stalls full of fruits, vegetables, cheeses, fish, art objects, and used clothing, he occasionally found a book about mathematics or physics. During one successful trip, he found two books from the mid-1800s, written in Latin.

Fermi met Enrico Persico, a boy one year older than himself who shared his strong interest in science and mathematics. Together, they searched for books at the marketplace of Campo dei Fiori, then shared them, analyzing scientific questions.

At age 17, Fermi took an examination in order to qualify for admission to the University of Pisa, a school that was highly regarded for its science curriculum. He earned an unusually high score and received a scholarship. One examiner was so amazed that such a young person received so high a score that he tested Fermi again, individually. After their conversation, the examiner said that Enrico Fermi was "exceptional."

At the University of Pisa, Fermi found himself in the town where his hero, Galileo, had once lived. There was a mood of relief and optimism in Italy in 1918. World War I was ending and Germany was defeated. Fermi and other young Italian men could plan their futures without worrying about wartime service.

Fermi received his doctoral degree in physics in July 1922, graduating with high honors. Not yet 21 years old, he had written a well-received paper on X rays. But the Italian government was changing. In October of that same year, Benito Mussolini came to power and instituted a Fascist dictatorship. Fermi was disturbed by these political events, but they did not affect him much personally during the 1920s.

Fermi got a government fellowship to study with the famous physicist Max Born at the University of Göttingen, in Germany. Born was known for his work with quantum mechanics, a new field that excited scientists around the world. After seven months in Göttingen, Fermi returned to Rome to teach mathematics to science students at the University of Rome.

Soon he was invited to study with prominent scientists at Leyden in the Netherlands. Fermi had been wondering about his abilities. Professors in Leyden convinced him that he showed great promise. In 1924, he returned to Italy to become a lecturer in math at the University of Florence. He continued to publish scientific papers, including some that dealt with theoretical physics, such as Einstein's theory of relativity.

Fermi was intrigued in 1925 when he read about the work of Austrian-born physicist Wolfgang Pauli. Pauli had stated the scientific principle that only one electron (negatively charged subatomic particle) can be found on each orbit around an atom's nucleus. Using Pauli's idea, the principle of exclusion, Fermi wrote an important paper on the nature of gases, a subject he had studied for several years. He developed calculations, known as Fermi's statistics, in order to predict the behavior of gases. Fermi and others later used these statistics to study the way in which metals conduct heat and electricity.

Fermi's work impressed physicists at the University of Rome. They asked him to join the faculty as the first professor of theoretical physics. Although Fermi focused on theories (ideas and predictions relating to the science), he also began to study experimental (applied) physics, hoping to learn as much as possible about the whole realm of this science.

Fermi was known as a gifted teacher who could explain complex theories in simple terms. He could also identify basic issues in a problem and rule out unrelated factors. He developed a strong reputation in his field, and so did the university's physics department, which attracted other talented professors and students.

Meanwhile, Fermi got to know Laura Capon, a second-year student in general science. They shared an interest in outdoor hiking, as well as science, and were married in the summer of 1928. The next year, Fermi was elected to the Royal Academy of Italy, becoming its youngest member. In 1930, he was invited to lecture at the University of Michigan in Ann Arbor. Writing about this trip, Laura Fermi described how hard she and her husband worked to learn English.

Enrico and Laura Fermi welcomed their first child, Nella, in 1931. Extraordinary events were also taking place in physics. In 1932, English scientist Sir James Chadwick had discovered the neutron, an electrically neutral particle found in the atom. He had also used rays from radium to knock the neutrons out of a metallic element called beryllium. Knowing that these rays were dangerous, Chadwick encased them in lead to keep the deadly radiation inside.

Experiments two years later by Frédéric and Irène Joliot-Curie extended this knowledge. The Joliot-Curies placed the element aluminum near a radioactive substance that was emitting tiny particles of atoms called alpha particles.* When these alpha particles struck (bombarded) the aluminum, the nuclei of the aluminum atoms also emitted particles—the bombardment had made them radioactive. The Joliot-Curies conducted more experiments and found that other light elements were likewise unstable and could be made to shoot off small particles during disintegration. The alpha ray bombardment had turned these materials radioactive, too.

Fermi published a paper on beta decay (radioactive beta ray disintegration) in 1934. He had been intrigued by the Joliot-Curie experiments and decided that he would produce artificial radioactivity himself, using neutrons. Because neutrons have no electrical charge, Fermi reasoned that they would not be attracted by negatively charged electrons around an atom nor repelled by its nucleus, as the alpha particles were. Because of these factors, Fermi predicted that more neutrons would reach their target—the nucleus—than alpha particles had.

Although the use of neutrons for bombardment experiments made sense, Fermi had not chosen an easy task. Neutrons were much harder to get than alpha particles, which are natural by-products of certain radioactive substances. Not only did Fermi need a source of neutrons, he needed a tool that would detect radioactivity. Today, Geiger counters are available for this purpose, but in the early 1930s Fermi had to build his own.

Luckily, Fermi knew a professor who worked in a physics laboratory that had some radium. The professor lent Fermi a precious gram of radium and a device to remove radon gas from it. When radium disintegrates, radon gas forms. Then the radon disintegrates, too, and emits alpha particles. Fermi knew that if he mixed radon with beryllium powder, alpha particles would strike the beryllium, releasing the neutrons he needed for his experiments.

---

*Alpha particles are helium nuclei, each composed of two protons and two neutrons, that have a positive charge. They are thus repelled by other positive charges, especially at close range. Heavier elements have stronger positive charges.

Next Fermi devised a neutron "gun"—a glass tube that held radioactive material and a small amount of beryllium. Particles from the radioactive material shot out, hitting the beryllium nuclei and sending out neutrons from the beryllium atoms. Fermi would use these neutron bullets to bombard different elements.

Thus with a small lab, little money, and some handmade equipment, Fermi began his 1934 tests. He tested elements on the periodic table of elements, starting with hydrogen, the lightest. Then came lithium, the next element he could obtain—then boron . . . carbon . . . nitrogen . . . Nothing happened until he tested fluorine. Then the Geiger counter began to click—fluorine had become radioactive! Fermi went on to produce radioactivity in elements heavier than fluorine. Eagerly, he and his research group bombarded element number 92 on the periodic table, uranium, then the heaviest of all atoms with its 92 protons. Uranium was highly radioactive, and Fermi found he had produced three known forms (isotopes) of uranium. But some of the uranium atoms had changed into a substance he could not identify. It was considered that this could be a new isotope of uranium, perhaps element number 93, but Fermi and his group did not want to draw any hasty, false conclusions. However, the news of these tests reached the press. Journalists wrote that a new element, number 93, had been produced. In America, a *New York Times* headline declared, "Italian Produces 93rd Element by Bombarding Uranium." According to his wife, Laura, "Fermi was disturbed. He did not like publicity." Besides, he wanted to conduct more tests before making any announcements. Fermi wrote a press release, saying that more studies were needed before it could be said that element 93 had been created.

Fermi did not know what had happened at that time, but he had split the uranium atom. Using his ideas, some German physicists would discover uranium fission in 1939.

Later that same year, Fermi and his associates tried something new: They enclosed a neutron source in paraffin (a waxy material used in making candles) and placed it in a hollow block of silver. The silver became more radioactive when it was bombarded in this manner because paraffin contains a large amount of hydrogen. Neutrons passing through the paraffin ran into hydrogen nuclei (protons, which have the same mass as do neutrons). This took away some of the neutrons' energy and slowed them down. These slower neutrons hit more targets while traveling through the silver, thus more neutrons were "captured" by the silver atoms.

Enrico Fermi

To check his theories, Fermi repeated these tests using water, which also contains much hydrogen. Water slowed down the neutrons, too. High levels of radioactivity resulted. Fermi concluded that "slow" neutrons made better bullets than ordinary, faster neutrons.

As Fermi made these exciting discoveries, he and Laura welcomed a son, Giulio, in 1936. But political changes threatened both his work and his family. Fascist governments now dominated Germany and Italy. The growing oppression by these governments endangered academic freedom and Jews, who were being cruelly persecuted in Hitler's Germany. Laura was Jewish, so the Fermis were especially concerned. After Mussolini and Hitler became allies, anti-Jewish laws were passed in Italy. Other laws dictated educational policies, behavior, and even the kinds of clothing people could wear.

Enrico Fermi had visited the United States several times during the 1930s. Many American universities had invited him to join their faculties, so he and Laura decided to leave Europe. Thus when Fermi received a phone call in November 1938 announcing that he had won the Nobel Prize for physics, he welcomed the honor for another reason: His family now had a convenient reason to leave Italy. Fermi would say that he was going to teach at Columbia University for six months, but they would stay in America.

Secretly, the Fermis made plans for their departure. To get permission to live in America, they had to pass examinations at the U.S. consulate in Rome. There, an examiner asked if Enrico Fermi, world-famous physicist, knew the sum of 15 and 27! "Forty-two," Fermi answered correctly.

In Sweden, on December 10, 1938, Fermi was awarded the Nobel Prize "for his identification of new radioactive elements produced by neutron bombardment, and his discovery, made in connection with this work, of nuclear reactions effected by slow neutrons." Back in Italy, government officials criticized Fermi for not greeting King Gustavus V of Sweden with a Fascist salute. But Fermi and his family were on a ship headed for America. As they approached New York Harbor, writes Laura Fermi, her husband said, "We have founded the American branch of the Fermi family."

In America, the Fermis settled in Leonia, New Jersey. Fermi began teaching at Columbia University. That same month, Niels Bohr arrived in America. Laura and Enrico Fermi welcomed the distinguished Danish physicist, who had fled from Denmark after it was invaded by Hitler's army.

Later, Fermi and Bohr discussed extraordinary news: An Austrian physicist, Lise Meitner, had been working in Berlin, Germany, with Otto Hahn and Frederic Strassman. They had bombarded elements using Fermi's 1934 methods. Being Jewish, Meitner left Germany. Hahn and Strassman continued to bombard uranium, analyzing the results. They were surprised to find barium, number 56 on the periodic table of elements, among the by-products of the reaction. Past tests of this kind had yielded protons, neutrons, and alpha particles. But all of those particles weigh far less than barium. Hahn and Strassman sent news to Meitner about these confusing results and published their findings in *Nature*, a British scientific journal.

Meitner was now in Copenhagen working with her nephew Otto Frisch, another refugee from Germany. They repeated the Hahn-Strassman tests. Meitner concluded that the uranium atoms were unstable—almost like liquid. They split and broke down into atoms of other elements, one of which was barium. Yet, all these new elements together had less mass than the original uranium atom, leaving the question of what had happened to the remaining mass. For the answer, Meitner turned to Albert Einstein, who had first suggested that matter contains energy. His famous equation, $E = mc^2$, means (in simple terms): Energy is equal to mass multiplied by the square of the velocity (speed) of light. Meitner thought she had the answer: The lost mass had turned into energy. She shared her interpretation with Niels Bohr, calling the splitting of the uranium atom *fission*. Meitner believed that the fragments of uranium flew apart at such high speed that they released tremendous energy in the process. As Bohr and Fermi talked about Meitner's theory, Fermi made figures and notations on paper, as was his habit. His wife recalls that he said,

It takes one neutron to split one atom of uranium. We must first produce and then use up that one neutron. Let's assume, however, that . . . an atom of uranium emits two neutrons. There would now be two neutrons available without the need of producing them. It is conceivable that they might hit two more atoms of uranium, split them, and make them emit two neutrons each. At the end of this second process of fission we would have four neutrons, which would split four atoms. After one more step, eight neutrons would be available and could split eight more atoms of uranium. . . . Starting with only a few man-produced neutrons to bombard a certain amount of uranium, we would be able to produce a set of *reactions that would continue spontaneously until all uranium atoms were split.*

Fermi was suggesting that a vast amount of uranium could be made to explode in a chain reaction. He thought that after the first neutron made an atom explode, other neutrons would be released. They, in turn, would split still more atoms, releasing larger amounts of energy. It now seemed possible to use the unlimited sources of atomic energy.

Perhaps this chain reaction was feasible; perhaps it was only a theory—but the prospect was frightening. Fission had occurred in Hitler's Germany. If the Nazis learned to use atomic energy, they might make deadly weapons and win the war.

Fermi and other scientists were excited about the challenge ahead. At Columbia, Fermi worked with a cyclotron, invented by physicist Ernest O. Lawrence at the University of California. The machine speeds up charged particles, such as protons, and keeps them moving in a circular path by means of a large magnet that bends the path of the particles. The particles stay inside a cylindrical box where they travel in circles at increasing speeds. Working with Herbert Anderson, Walter H. Zinn, Leo Szilard, and others, Fermi used the particles that came from the cyclotron to bombard elements and produce neutrons.

With the cyclotron providing neutrons, Fermi went on to the problem of how to get a steady release of energy and keep it going. He believed a large pile of uranium would let neutrons hit enough targets to start a chain reaction. Nobody was sure what size that pile should be.

As Fermi and his team worked on these problems, the war in Europe widened. Hungarian-born scientist Leo Szilard suggested that a group of scientists write to President Roosevelt asking the U.S. government to fund their research. This letter, with Einstein's signature, convinced the president. With more funds, Fermi bought graphite, a material that would slow down the speeding neutrons in his pile. Pure graphite and pure uranium were difficult to get. During 1940 and 1941, these materials were gathered and purified so that they could be used in a future chain reaction. Fermi worked with small amounts of materials to predict what might happen later. He began to arrive home with black hands and clothing but could not explain his appearance because the work was now secret.

Nobel laureate Arthur H. Compton of the University of Chicago was asked to coordinate research to develop a chain reaction. Fermi began commuting back and forth from New York to Chicago. Soon the project needed a larger space and was moved to a squash court under the West Stands at the university's Stagg Field Stadium. The room was 30 feet wide, 60 feet long, and 26 feet high.

Enrico Fermi, at work in the classroom, illustrating a lecture on physics.
(Courtesy of the Argonne National Laboratory)

Fermi used the small pile at Columbia University to get information that would apply to a larger pile. As the Chicago pile grew, Fermi estimated what size would produce a chain reaction. Control rods made out of cadmium were embedded into the pile. These rods prevented neutrons from reaching the uranium that was placed at intervals among the graphite bricks. Removing the rods would let the neutrons pass through.

The scientists worked under pressure as fears increased during 1941 that Germany might harness atomic energy first. Nazi troops now controlled a factory in occupied Norway—the only large factory in the world producing what was known as heavy water. U.S. scientists feared that Germany planned to use heavy water to slow down neutrons in a chain reaction. In America, Harold Urey was producing heavy water, too, in case it was needed to develop atomic energy. After Pearl Harbor was bombed on December 7, 1941, the United States was at war with Japan as well as with the Fascist allied nations. Still more American scientists began conducting military research.

The nuclear chain reaction project had been moved to Chicago, and the Fermis relocated there in mid-1942. The pile at the squash court continued to rise, its floor black and slippery from graphite dust. The scientists wore overalls and goggles as they worked. Soon a lattice wall of black bricks with small spaces in between them stretched almost to the ceiling. Fermi checked various instruments placed inside the pile that recorded the actions of the neutrons traveling through the carbon.

Finally, Fermi concluded that the pile was large enough to test for a chain reaction. Nineteen men and one woman, physicist Leona Wood, witnessed the dramatic event. Some feared the pile might be uncontrollable, releasing deadly radiation, or that it might explode. Three young men (jokingly called the "suicide squad") were atop the pile, beside buckets full of a cadmium solution that would absorb neutrons in case of a fire. Physicist George Weil stood beside the pile, ready to pull out the cadmium rods. As Fermi gave the word, Weil climbed up and began to withdraw 13-foot-long cadmium control rods.

Fermi's wife recorded the participants' memories of that day:

There was utter silence in the audience, and only Fermi spoke. His gray eyes betrayed his intense thinking and his hands moved along with his thoughts. . . . As he spoke, others acted. Each chore had been assigned in advance and rehearsed. . . . He said, "Presently we shall begin our experiment. George will pull out his rod a little at a time. We shall take measurements and verify that the pile will keep on acting as we have calculated." Fermi anticipated that the Geiger counters would click faster and a pen attached to the reaction would trace a line indicating its intensity. Then he said, "Go ahead, George." Eyes turned to the graph pen. Breathing was suspended. Fermi grinned with confidence. The counters stepped up their clicking; the pen went up and then stopped where Fermi had said it would. . . . Each time Weil pulled the rod out some more, the counters increased the rate of their clicking. And then, those present said that Fermi announced, "Let's go to lunch." (After lunch, they went on with the experiment.) At 3:20, Fermi told Weil to "pull it out another foot." A chain reaction occurred in the pile, as was clear from the activity of the Geiger counters and the pen rising upward. The "suicide squad" was ready for any accidents, but none occurred. The pile behaved as it should, as they all had hoped that it would, as they had feared it would not.

Nuclear physicists at Los Alamos at one of their weekly scientific meetings. Fermi is second from right, Robert Oppenheimer at left in the second row.
(Courtesy of Los Alamos National Laboratory)

"We have a chain reaction," said Fermi. He allowed it to go on for 28 minutes, then instructed his staff to push the control rods back into the pile. Hungarian-born physicist Eugene Wigner gave Fermi a bottle of red Italian wine. The observers toasted their triumph in paper cups and signed their names on the straw casing around the bottle, providing a record of the persons who had been there that day. They had just seen that energy could be produced by splitting atoms and that such a flow of energy could be controlled.

After the successful chain reaction, work on atomic weapons proceeded more rapidly. The scientific director of the bomb-building project, Robert Oppenheimer, organized a team at Los Alamos, New Mexico. Fermi was an obvious choice to join this group. Under the code name Eugene Farmer, he arrived at Los Alamos in August 1944 and spent a year directing a theory unit of the Manhattan Project to build the atomic bomb. Also in 1944, he and Laura became U.S. citizens.

Fermi was among those who witnessed the unprecedented, brilliant flash of light over the New Mexico desert at dawn on July 16, 1945. As the first atomic bomb exploded, Fermi was busy dropping small pieces of paper on the ground. Air blasts from the eruption blew the papers away. By measuring the distance they fell from him, Fermi calculated the power of the explosion. Later, he found that his calculations agreed with those recorded by instruments during the explosion.

Atomic bombs were dropped on the Japanese cities of Hiroshima and Nagasaki on August 6 and August 9, less than a month after the test in New Mexico. In the history of science, it has been rare that the results of research are put into use so quickly.

Fermi's wife wrote that he disliked the idea that Japanese civilians had been killed and injured but thought things would have been worse had the enemy gotten the atomic bomb first. Fermi thought that, throughout history, the development of stronger weapons had not seemed to deter wars.

Enrico Fermi also pointed out that in previous centuries, science had been a quiet, often solitary pursuit. Many scientists had contributed knowledge without considering how it would be used by others. Fermi told his students how, when the Italian scientist Allessandro Volta was working on electricity, he had no way to know its eventual effects. Similarly, scientists at Los Alamos worked apart from other members of society, toward a common goal. Fermi said that they hoped they could end the war quickly.

After the war ended, Fermi no longer wanted to work on military weapons. He returned to the University of Chicago in 1946 to conduct research and teach. Fermi believed that it was essential to inspire new generations of scientists. That year, he received the Congressional Medal of Merit. General Leslie Groves, who had been connected with the Manhattan Project, said that Fermi was a "great experimental physicist" and that "Dr. Fermi's sound scientific judgment, his initiative and resourcefulness, and his unswerving devotion to duty have contributed vitally to the success of the Atomic Bomb project."

Fermi continued to study the nucleus, or core of the atom. He helped to plan the new giant "atom smasher" cyclotron at the University of Chicago. It was finished in 1951 and was placed inside the Accelerator Building across from the West Stands at Stagg Field. Fermi also designed a device that became known as "Fermi's Trolley": a plastic wheeled carrier that runs around the rim of the cyclotron, enabling scientists to move equipment. This safety device lets the operators control the trolley while staying farther away from radiation emitted by the cyclotron.

December 1947: Chancellor Hutchins of the University of Chicago unveils a plaque commemorating the first controlled nuclear chain reaction. In attendance are some members of the team that conducted the test on December 2, 1942, from left to right: Walter H. Zinn, Sumner T. Pike, Robert F. Bacher, Samuel K. Allison, Farrington Daniels, William W. Waymack, Enrico Fermi.
(Courtesy of the University of Chicago)

Enrico Fermi

In 1946, Fermi received the title Distinguished Service Professor of Physics at the Institute of Nuclear Studies at the University of Chicago. He continued to study basic properties of nuclear particles, focusing on mesons, which help to hold the nucleus together. He also joined scientists and others who opposed the hydrogen bomb on ethical grounds.

In 1950, he was elected to the Royal Society of London as a foreign member. Fermi became the first person to receive a special award given by the U.S. Atomic Energy Commission. The award, given to him in November 1954, included $25,000.

That same year, Fermi had traveled to Europe to meet with other scientists, but he returned home quite ill. On November 28, 1954, he died of cancer of the stomach at the age of only 53. In his honor, the Atomic Energy Commission now gives its annual Enrico Fermi Award to the person who has contributed the most to the "development, use, or control of atomic energy." The University of Chicago Institute of Nuclear Physics was also renamed the Enrico Fermi Institute for Nuclear Studies. Enrico Fermi might also have been pleased when, in 1955, a new element, fermium, was named in his honor. A radioactive element, fermium is part of the group known as transuranium elements and is number 100 on the periodic table.

People who knew Enrico Fermi often commented on his sense of humor. When a new laboratory was being built at the University of Chicago, it is said that Fermi saw a sketch of a sculpture to be placed at the entrance. He joked that the sketch was probably of a scientist who was *not* discovering fission.

Although Fermi did not know that he had produced nuclear fission in 1934, he went on to give the world atomic energy. It was Fermi who figured out how to make a pile of uranium atoms split and continue to split, resulting in the first controlled nuclear chain reaction. Although this power was first used for weapons of war, nuclear reactors now provide energy for peaceful purposes all over the world. Nuclear devices are also used in medicine, for example, to treat cancer. Like some of the other astonishing discoveries of the 20th century, the use of nuclear power is the subject of much debate.

After watching Fermi direct the first nuclear chain reaction in 1942, Arthur Compton telephoned a friend with the news, saying in carefully coded language, "The Italian navigator has reached the new world." Indeed he had—and so had humankind.

Chronology

September 29, 1901	Enrico Fermi born in Rome, Italy
1918	enters the University of Pisa
1922	receives Ph.D. in physics; awarded a fellowship to work at the University of Göttingen in Germany
1926	publishes important paper on the nature of gases and becomes first professor of theoretical physics at the University of Rome
1929	elected as the youngest member of the Royal Academy of Italy
1934	publishes paper on beta ray disintegration; begins neutron bombardment experiments to produce radioactivity artificially; unknowingly produces fission of the uranium atom
1938	awarded the Nobel Prize in physics and emigrates with his wife and two children to America
1939	learns about the Hahn-Strassman nuclear fission experiments and envisions the potential for a chain reaction; with other scientists, he seeks government funding for nuclear research
1940–41	heads the scientific team working to develop a nuclear pile
December 2, 1942	directs the first controlled self-sustaining nuclear chain reaction at the University of Chicago
1944–45	directs a unit of theoretical physicists working on the

	Manhattan Project at Los Alamos, New Mexico
1944	becomes a U.S. citizen
1945	returns to teach at the University of Chicago after the bomb project is completed with successful tests in July
1946	receives Congressional Medal of Merit and is named Distinguished Service Professor for Nuclear Studies at the University of Chicago; consultant to the building of the university's large particle accelerator
1950	elected as foreign member to the Royal Society of London
1954	chosen as first recipient of special award (renamed the Fermi Award after his death) from the U.S. Atomic Energy Commission
November 24, 1954	Enrico Fermi dies at age 53

Further Reading

Fermi, Laura. *Atoms in the Family: My Life with Enrico Fermi.* Chicago: University of Chicago Press, 1954. A comprehensive and lively biography of the physicist by his widow, with clear explanations of his scientific work.

———. *The Story of Atomic Energy* New York: Random House, 1961. History of important scientific work that led to the development of atomic power and its various military and peaceful uses.

Gallant, Roy A. *Explorers of the Atom.* Garden City, New York: Doubleday, 1974. Discusses scientists who studied the atom, contributing to the steady growth of knowledge about its structure and function.

Silverberg, Robert. *Men Who Mastered the Atom.* New York: G.P. Putnam's Sons, 1965. Traces the history of key discoveries about the atom and atomic power.

Heathcote, Niels H. de V. *Breakthroughs in Twentieth Century Science: Nobel Prize Winners in Physics 1901–1950.* New York: Henry Schuman, Inc., 1953. Portraits of famous physicists, describing the work that enabled them to win this high scientific honor.

Robert Oppenheimer: Building the Atomic Bomb

Robert Oppenheimer.
(Courtesy of Los Alamos National Laboratory)

*A*t an isolated desert near Alamogordo, New Mexico, just before dawn, on July 16, 1945, the countdown began: Zero minus 25 seconds . . . zero minus 15 seconds . . . zero minus ten seconds . . . At that point, a flare, bright green in color, was sent up. The flare was meant as a warning to the hundreds of people waiting in the desert that they must not look at the sky without wearing the special shaded glasses they had been given. The world's first atomic bomb was about to be tested and a blinding light, too dangerous for unprotected eyes, was expected.

Robert Oppenheimer, the scientific director of the team that had developed the bomb, put on his glasses. According to one person at the scene, Oppenheimer "scarcely breathed. He held on to a post to steady himself" as he watched from the trench where he waited along with other silent bystanders.

The bomb exploded at 5:25:45 A.M., Rocky Mountain Time. The burst of light, which witnesses later called indescribably intense, was followed by a huge roaring noise. An enormous, mushroomlike cloud spiraled its way 41,000 feet above the desert floor.

General Thomas Farrell, a brigadier general in the Army Air Force, later reported his observations to the U.S. War Department:

> *The whole country was lighted by a searching light with the intensity many times that of the midday sun. It was golden, purple, violet, gray, and blue. It lighted every peak, crevasse, and ridge of the near-by mountain range with a clarity and beauty that cannot be described. . . . Thirty seconds after the explosion came first the air blast, pressing hard against the people and things; to be followed almost immediately by the strong, sustained, awesome roar which warned of doomsday . . .*

Other witnesses described the light as an ugly greenish hue, which changed to orange, then to shades of violet and lavender, finally reflecting the orange-gold color of the rising sun. They spoke of the weird patterns made by the rising smoke and clouds. In cities more than one hundred miles from Alamogordo, people felt the earth shaking as a result of the explosion.

The test, called Trinity, was the result of months of concentrated, hurried research. Scientists from all over the United States and from several other countries had joined forces to do the demanding work that led to this bomb. At a secret site in Los Alamos, New Mexico, the American physicist Robert Oppenheimer had coordinated the efforts of these hundreds of scientists and technicians.

Now the nuclear age had truly begun. As he watched, Oppenheimer found himself recalling an ancient Hindu phrase: "I am become Death, the destroyer of worlds." Oppenheimer knew that this bomb was meant to be a weapon of war. Like other scientists who had worked on this project, he was concerned about the human suffering that could result. Yet these scientists and top U.S. government officials had agreed that they must build atomic weapons. For more than five years, World War II had caused terrible destruction and millions of deaths. By building atomic weapons first, the Allies hoped to end the war. As scientific director of that work, Robert Oppenheimer had assumed a tremendous responsibility.

━━━━━━━━

Robert Oppenheimer was born on April 22, 1904, in New York City. His father, Julius Oppenheimer, had moved there from Hanau, Germany, in 1888, to work in his uncle's cloth importing business. Seventeen-year-old Julius learned English quickly. An avid reader, he enjoyed music, literature, art, and science. His frequent visits to art exhibits led to a meeting with his future wife. Ella Friedman was an artist and teacher who had been born in the United States, also part of a European-Jewish family.

By age 32, Julius had prospered in the textile business. He and Ella were married in 1903. Robert, their first son, was born in 1904. Later, the family gave Robert an additional name, Julius, and he was commonly known as J. Robert Oppenheimer.

Oppenheimer had a comfortable childhood with loving parents and many cultural advantages. He visited Europe during his early years. On one visit, when he was five years old, Oppenheimer's German grandfather gave him a mineral collection, which sparked the boy's interest in science.

Science was just one of many subjects that Oppenheimer explored during his youth. At various times, he planned to have a career in art, poetry, and architecture. He showed an amazing ability to recall long passages from books he had read and music he had heard. People were also impressed by his advanced vocabulary.

The School for Ethical Culture, an innovative private school in New York City, helped Oppenheimer to develop his wide-ranging interests. The school worked to teach values and morals that are shared by cultures throughout the world. Besides reading, writing, and mathematics, there were courses in languages, the arts, literature, and philosophy. In science classes, students could observe and experiment using a hands-on approach to learning. Oppenheimer liked science and began to study physics in the fifth grade.

Oppenheimer was a shy and physically frail child who was more comfortable studying or pursuing quiet hobbies. He was not athletic until he took up sailing during his teens. He later said that he was more at ease with adults than with other children. But he did enjoy the company of his younger brother, Frank, born in 1912.

At age 12, Robert presented his first scientific paper in public, although quite by accident. He had continued to study rocks and minerals through the years, collecting specimens from various places. Oppenheimer used a typewriter to correspond with geologists in different states. One of them proposed that Robert Oppenheimer be accepted as a member of the New York Mineralogical Society. Members were so impressed by his letters that Oppenheimer was invited to present a paper at a meeting of the society. Oppenheimer was embarrassed and wanted to refuse, but his parents convinced him that he would do well. That night, members of the society were surprised to find that their speaker was not yet in high school!

As a high school student, Oppenheimer continued to excel in the sciences, doing college-level work. He astonished teachers by completing a year-long chemistry course in only six weeks. Besides, he found time to learn five modern languages, as well as Greek and Latin. Oppenheimer later described himself as a bookworm whose favorite activities were reading, writing poetry, building things, and working on his mineral collection. When he graduated in 1921, Oppenheimer was valedictorian of his high school class.

Robert Oppenheimer was accepted at Harvard University and had planned to start school that fall. He had reached a height of six feet but was very thin and still shy around his peers. The summer after high school, Oppenheimer became sick with dysentery, an illness of the digestive system. Doctors advised him to go to a warm, dry climate, so his parents asked Herbert Smith, his athletic, outgoing chemistry teacher, to accompany their son on a trip to the American Southwest. Oppenheimer visited a dude ranch in New Mexico. He developed a lifelong love of horseback riding and the rugged desert country, where he hiked and camped.

At Harvard, Oppenheimer took many science courses, mostly chemistry. He continued to excel in Latin, Greek, and philosophy, including Oriental studies. Some of his poems and stories were published in the college literary magazine, *Hound and Horn*. Other students noticed his brilliant mind and superb ability to concentrate.

Although he was a chemistry major, Oppenheimer became excited by physics after taking a course in thermodynamics (the study of how heat is used to generate power). He found that he excelled at scientific theory but not at laboratory work. His physics professor, Dr. Percy Bridgman, concluded that Oppenheimer would make his mark as a theoretical, not an experimental, physicist.

Oppenheimer took only three years, instead of the usual four, to graduate, summa cum laude (with high honors). He received his bachelor's degree in 1925 and won a fellowship to study physics at the famous Cavendish Laboratory in Cambridge, England. It was then headed by Ernest Rutherford. A Nobel laureate, Rutherford was famous for his studies of radiation and his work on the theory of the atom as being a nucleus surrounded by a cloud of electrons. Rutherford attracted top-notch scientists to work at Cavendish.

In Europe, Oppenheimer found that his physics classes demanded more knowledge of chemistry and mathematics. He mastered the material on his own. As before, he was awkward in the laboratory but outstanding in analysis. Sensitive about this shortcoming, Oppenheimer once wrote to a friend: "The lab work is terrible, and I am so bad at it that it is impossible to feel I am learning anything." Like Albert Einstein, Robert Oppenheimer was more comfortable coming up with ideas and theories, mentally or with chalk or pencil.

As he had been in the United States, Oppenheimer was a loner in Europe. He was ill at ease in many social settings, and some of his fellow students thought he had a superior attitude, especially toward less intelligent people. For a time, his close friends worried about his moodiness and other signs of depression. They encouraged him to enjoy leisure activities, including a summer hiking trip across the continent. By the time the hiking vacation ended, Oppenheimer appeared cheerful again.

Oppenheimer was invited to study at the University of Göttingen by Max Born, the prominent physicist who headed this world famous research center. Born allowed Oppenheimer to pursue theoretical studies. In later years, Born said, "Oppenheimer seemed to me right from the beginning a very gifted man." Born also saw Oppenheimer as a philosopher who was trying to understand science "as part of the general intellectual development in the course of human history."

Despite his full schedule, Oppenheimer found time to learn Italian and Dutch. He became more sociable and began dating a woman who was also studying physics at Göttingen. His fellow students grew to know him as a generous person who was more shy than snobbish.

Robert Oppenheimer wrote several scientific papers, alone and with other scientists, about his research. His doctoral paper discussed some newly developing theories in quantum mechanics. In 1926, he collaborated with Max Born on a paper about the energy levels of molecules. The paper was widely praised and quoted in textbooks, journals, and lectures. Other papers written by Oppenheimer proposed original ideas, which were tested and verified by different experimental scientists.

When he was granted his doctoral degree from Göttingen in 1927, at the age of only 23, Oppenheimer received several good job offers from American universities. But while visiting his family in New York, Oppenheimer again became ill. The doctors thought his coughing might be caused by tuberculosis, a lung disease. They suggested that he return to the West for the warm, dry weather. Oppenheimer and his brother, Frank, bought a log cabin in the Sangre de Cristo mountains of New Mexico. They called their vacation house Perro Caliente—"hot dog" in Spanish.

By 1928, Oppenheimer felt well enough to continue his studies, first at the University of Leyden, in the Netherlands, then at the Technical Institute in Zurich, Switzerland. Just six weeks after he arrived in Leyden, Oppenheimer gave a lecture in Dutch. His Dutch friends gave him the affectionate nickname "Opje." Later, the spelling became Americanized to "Oppie."

In spring 1929, Oppenheimer went to Zurich. There, he made friends with Felix Bloch, a Swiss native who would win the 1952 Nobel Prize in physics. Bloch later praised the broad scope of Oppenheimer's interests, saying, "He was not a man one could exhaust with a simple formula." Bloch also noted that Oppenheimer spoke often about his love for America. Oppenheimer later wrote, "In the spring of 1929, I returned to the United States. I was homesick for this country, and in fact did not leave it again for nineteen years. I had learned a great deal in my student days about the new physics; I wanted to pursue this myself, to explain it, and to foster its cultivation. . . ."

The science of physics had expanded rapidly during the 1920s. The new theories of quantum physics and Einstein's theory of relativity had changed the direction of thinking and research. These dramatic movements in physics had been accomplished by European scientists. Now some talented Americans, including Robert Oppenheimer, were ready to make important contributions. Oppenheimer devoted his early research to the study of subatomic particles, those minute bits of mass that are part of the atom, such as electrons and positrons. Between 1926 and 1929, Oppenheimer published 16 papers dealing with quantum physics.

With his impressive credentials Oppenheimer obtained an attractive position: He was jointly appointed to the University of California at Berkeley and to the California Institute of Technology (Caltech) in Pasadena. He would teach at both places and help to develop programs to teach the "new physics."

Oppenheimer was not an immediate success as a professor. Students complained that he smoked continually and that his lectures were too difficult for them to understand. Realizing that he was not reaching his students, Oppenheimer changed his style of teaching. He worked to make his presentations more clear and met with students individually when they had problems in class. He also became a friend and role model, inviting students to special meals he had prepared, often with a southwestern menu. He began to enjoy discussing science, philosophy, and other topics with young people.

As Oppenheimer's reputation grew, more students came to California in order to study with him. Oppenheimer continued to explore theoretical physics. In 1928, a British physicist, Paul Dirac, had proposed that there was a particle in the atom called an anti-electron. Oppenheimer studied Dirac's theory, then calculated the mass and the weight of the anti-electron (now called a positron). Working at Caltech, American physicist Carl D. Anderson found such a particle while doing cosmic ray research, confirming Oppenheimer's formula.

Oppenheimer and other physicists contributed ideas about elementary particles that led to a greater understanding of the behavior of atoms. While studying cosmic rays, Oppenheimer concluded that the Japanese scientist Hideki Yukawa had been right when he declared that there was yet another subatomic particle, the meson. Again, Carl D. Anderson detected such particles while analyzing cosmic rays.

Before the 1930s, Oppenheimer had shown slight interest in politics. He did not own a radio or telephone nor did he read daily newspapers. But dramatic and frightening events taking place throughout the world heightened his social concern. In Europe, Austrian-born Adolf Hitler and his Nazi political party had gained power in Germany. Hitler became that country's dictator in 1933. He had a fanatical hatred of Jews and began to ruthlessly persecute them in Germany. Among these victims were prominent teachers, businesspeople, scientists, and others.

Oppenheimer helped his relatives to leave Germany. He worked with other American scientists who were raising money to help Jewish scientists and teachers to escape from Nazi oppression. These refugees had to leave everything behind. They needed jobs, housing, and sponsors in America.

Also in the 1930s, Oppenheimer was deeply moved by the poverty he saw as a result of the Great Depression. Millions of Americans lost their jobs; there were homeless and hungry people all over the nation. A drought caused more problems for people living in the areas of the Great Plains that came to be known as the dust bowl. Jobless migrants streamed into California, desperate to find farm work. Schools cut back on teachers and programs, and many students had to quit college. Oppenheimer gave some students money so they could stay in school. He later said, "I began to understand how deeply political and economic events could affect men's lives. I began to feel the need to participate more fully in the life of the community."

During the depression, Americans heard about political systems that offered different solutions for the nation's problems and promised to help disadvantaged people. Some people joined Socialist or Communist party groups or attended their meetings. Robert Oppenheimer had friends and colleagues who were members of these political groups. His brother, Frank, and Jean Tatlock, whom he dated seriously during the 1930s, had joined the Communist party, but Oppenheimer never did. Later, when he heard about the repressive tactics of Soviet Russia, he expressed a distaste for communism.

In 1939, as Oppenheimer proudly attended the commencement exercises at which Frank Oppenheimer received a Ph.D. in physics from Caltech, World War II continued to expand. Hitler's troops had invaded Czechoslovakia and Poland. Poland's allies, England and France, declared war on Germany. People worried that Hitler planned to conquer all of Europe.

Then came remarkable scientific news from Germany. Oppenheimer was among those who heard that German physicists had split the uranium atom in Berlin in 1939. Felix Bloch had fled from Europe and was working at Stanford University when Oppenheimer telephoned to say, "You must come to Berkeley immediately. There is something of the utmost importance I must show you."

When Bloch walked into Oppenheimer's office, his friend announced, "They have discovered fission."

In May 1939, another refugee scientist, Hungarian-born Leo Szilard, asked Albert Einstein to sign a letter warning the U.S. government that the Nazis might build a nuclear bomb. President Roosevelt set up a committee to study the issue. In October, the president got another letter signed by Einstein, asking for "unlimited funds" for research and development.

Throughout America, scientists and students conducted tests to verify the results obtained in Germany. Glenn Seaborg, a Nobel Prize–winning physicist, was one of Oppenheimer's students at that time. He recalls that fission was the subject of many excited seminars at the University of California.

During that eventful period, Robert Oppenheimer met Katherine Puening Harrison (called Kitty) at Berkeley, where she was doing post-graduate work in plant physiology. They were married in 1940 and bought a home, decorating it with fine furniture and art from Oppenheimer's collection. Oppenheimer had inherited his father's estate in 1937 and had a comfortable income beyond his teaching salary. In 1941, he and Kitty welcomed a son, Peter. Oppenheimer enjoyed caring for the baby and was often seen reading books about child-rearing and pediatrics.

That autumn, Arthur H. Compton asked Oppenheimer to attend a meeting in Chicago to discuss military uses of atomic energy. A special committee had been set up for this purpose through the National Academy of Sciences. Shortly thereafter, on December 7, the Japanese bombed Pearl Harbor, killing thousands of people and destroying U.S. naval ships. Now the United States was also at war in what had become a global conflict.

In the spring of 1942, Compton talked with Oppenheimer again, about the progress made toward developing atomic weapons. Scientists working on the nuclear chain reaction were optimistic. Compton had established a timetable that called for a sustained chain reaction by January 1943. A uranium processing plant began operating in Oak Ridge, Tennessee. Other research was being done all over the country.

Compton said that the work should be coordinated and asked if Oppenheimer would be willing to take on this role. Oppenheimer agreed, and he became the director of atomic research at the Office of Scientific Research and Development.

Major General Leslie R. Groves was appointed head of the nonscientific aspects of the bomb project. He was an engineer as well as a high-ranking army officer. Groves was known for his ability to complete difficult projects on schedule and within the budget. After meeting with several prominent scientists, Groves said that he liked Oppenheimer's ability to explain complex information in a way that he could understand.

One night in fall 1942, Oppenheimer was awakened by a telephone call from Groves, who had flown in from Washington, D.C., to meet with him. He wanted Oppenheimer to supervise the secret project to build the atomic bomb. Groves later wrote that he chose Oppenheimer because of his brilliant work in theoretical physics and "because I was unable to find anyone else who was available who I felt would do as well."

It was a strange undertaking for a man who had always considered himself a pacifist (a person opposed to war and violence). Yet Oppenheimer loathed the murderous acts of the Nazis and wanted to stop them, so he accepted Groves's offer. In order to be approved for this top-secret work, Oppenheimer had to pass an FBI security check. He received the security clearance.

On an overnight train ride to New York City, Groves, his aides, and Oppenheimer sat inside a locked compartment. They decided to find a central location where the major scientists needed for the project could work. This would strengthen communication and teamwork and reduce the security problems.

Science was to play a decisive role in the world events that followed. Knowledge and research became vital tools used by the Allies on one hand and the Nazis, Fascists and Japanese on the other. Hitler had boasted about the fierce weapons he was developing in order to defeat the Allies. In America, professors, researchers, and government officials united to outdo the enemy.

Oppenheimer joined Groves in New Mexico, where the army owned land at the White Sands Missile Range. By jeep, they hunted for a work site and chose a place called Los Alamos. It was a few miles west of Santa Fe, set amid deep, jagged canyons. Los Alamos was isolated, yet not too far from Santa Fe or Albuquerque, where they could go by car or public transportation to buy supplies. And Oppenheimer's Perro Caliente ranch was about 60 miles away. The U.S. government bought about 9,000 acres of land at Los Alamos for $415,000.

Throughout the 1942–43 winter, army crews built electrical and water lines, roads, labs, machinery shops, meeting rooms, and housing. About 4,500 people would live at Los Alamos during the next two years in these "barracks," painted green to blend with the surrounding hills and pine trees.

While the town in the desert took shape, Oppenheimer worked from offices in downtown Santa Fe. For secrecy, he was called "Mr. Bradley." Oppenheimer had stopped wearing his customary Stetson hat, which General Groves said was too noticeable. He began to wear the brownish-colored pork pie hat that became a trademark.

Robert Oppenheimer faced the most formidable challenge that a government had ever given to a scientist. First, he had to recruit top scientists and coordinate their work, then define research goals and priorities and schedule the steps in the building of the bomb. He also had to figure out what manpower and materials would be needed by Project Y—by then called the Manhattan Project or Manhattan Engineer District of the War Department.

Besides, Oppenheimer had to function as diplomat and counselor while directing the project. He needed to blend a diverse group of people, some used to working alone, into an effective team. Oppenheimer was able to maintain the morale of his staff. None of the scientists resigned or suffered a physical or mental breakdown while working on this stressful project.

The scientific questions facing Oppenheimer's team were vast and complex. Victor S. Weisskopf, a major theoretical physicist on the project, later wrote,

> *When the work started at Los Alamos not much more was known than the fundamental ideas of a chain reaction. What happens in a nuclear explosion had to be predicted theoretically in all its aspects for the design of the bomb, since there was no time to wait for experiments; no fissionable material was available yet. The details of the fission process had to be understood. The slowing down of neutrons in matter and the theory of explosions and implosions under completely novel conditions had to be investigated. Nuclear physicists had to become experts in fields of physics and technology unknown to them . . . Oppenheimer directed these studies in the real sense of the word. Here his uncanny speed in grasping the main points of any subject was a decisive factor; he could acquaint himself with the essential details of every part of the work.*

Oppenheimer recruited distinguished scientists to build the bomb—not an easy job, because he was asking them to work hard, in a remote southwestern desert, for relatively low pay. But the scientists trusted Oppenheimer. After the new recruits got their security clearances, he was able to tell them exactly what they would be doing at Los Alamos. Among those who came were such scientific giants as Enrico Fermi, James Chadwick (the man who discovered the neutron), Otto Frisch, Ernest Lawrence, Harold Urey, Hans Bethe, Emilio Segre, Edward Teller, and John von Neumann. Most of them were younger than 40, among them were some of Oppenheimer's former students. Most were Americans, but other countries were well represented. Some of the foreign scientists had escaped from Nazi Europe, including a gray-haired Dane with the code name "Nicholas Baker," whom some people called "Uncle Nick." He was Niels Bohr, regarded by many as the most famous physicist alive. Both he and his son Aage worked on the Manhattan Project.

Oppenheimer set up four main work units at Los Alamos: experimental physics, theoretical physics, chemistry and metallurgy (to test metals and decide what kinds should be used for the bomb), and ordnance (explosives). After a successful chain reaction had been produced in Chicago in December 1942, a large factory was built in Hanford, Washington. About 75,000 people worked there to process plutonium for the bomb. An isotope of uranium, U-235, was being produced for another type of bomb that was also being designed.

During the tense two and a half years at Los Alamos, Robert Oppenheimer worked six days a week and slept about four hours a night, continually making difficult decisions. According to Enrico Fermi's wife, Laura, who lived at Los Alamos and later wrote about the experience, "Oppie turned out to be a marvelous director, the real soul of the project. In his quiet, unobtrusive way, he kept informed about everything and in touch with everyone. His profound understanding of all phases of research—experimental, theoretical, technical—permitted him to coordinate them into a coherent whole and to accelerate the work."

Because Oppenheimer had lured such a famous "first team" of scientists, others agreed to follow. Eventually, there were 1,500 scientists, engineers, and technicians at Los Alamos. Their children attended a school there. There were 208 babies born to families working on the Manhattan Project, including Oppenheimer's daughter, Katherine, born in 1944. Living conditions were rough and the work hard, but the people at Los Alamos also described feelings of excitement and fellowship there. The staff was working toward a goal that they viewed as vitally important.

By 1944, Oppenheimer thought that there would be enough fissionable material (plutonium 239 or U-235) ready by spring 1945. It had taken a year to process the first ounce of plutonium, which arrived at Los Alamos in mid-1944. Oppenheimer's team had planned a uranium bomb that looked promising. It would require about 30–40 pounds of uranium. A chunk of U-235 would be shot out of a "gun" toward a second chunk of uranium at a speed faster than a bullet from a typical revolver. This would set a chain reaction in motion, with subsequent nuclear fission and explosion.

A plutonium bomb would not fission with the gun/bullet method. George Kistiakowsky, a Russian-born chemist from Harvard University, worked with British scientist Jim Tuck and others to develop another way of triggering a chain reaction. It combined standard explosives with plutonium so that blasts were sent inward and outward at the same time.

In August 1944, Oppenheimer told General Groves that three bombs could be ready by late summer 1945: one uranium gun bomb (known as Little Boy) and two plutonium bombs (called Fat Man, because of the shape). Oppenheimer appeared tired and anxious. At 6 feet 2 inches, he then weighed only 110 pounds.

On May 7, 1945, Germany surrendered, but Japan continued the war. The Manhattan Project stayed on schedule. On July 5, Oppenheimer sent a telegram to Arthur H. Compton in Chicago: "Anytime after the 15th would be a good time for our fishing trip. Because we are not certain of the weather, we may be delayed several days. As we do not have enough sleeping bags to go around, we ask that you do not bring anyone with you." In other words, the bomb would soon be tested. Oppenheimer had chosen a site at Alamogordo: There were no towns nearby, and security seemed excellent. The site, Trinity, was about 210 miles from Los Alamos.

Crews went to Alamogordo on Saturday, July 14th, to assemble the Fat Man (plutonium bomb) for the test two days later. The bomb's plutonium core was carried on a stretcher from a nearby building to the test site, or Ground Zero. The core was put together cautiously to prevent a premature chain reaction, which would emit deadly radiation. Geiger counters kept track of the radiation levels while the crew was at work.

Slowly, a crane lifted the assembled core over the center of the bomb. Then an unexpected problem arose: The core did not fit inside the bomb. Scientist Robert Bacher guessed that the live plutonium had produced such intense heat that the metal in the core expanded. Later, the core became cool enough to fit in place. Fat Man was egg-shaped and weighed about five tons. It was more than 12 feet high and five feet wide. Using pulleys, a crew lifted the bomb to the top of the 100-foot-high tower.

The crew worked all day, preparing for the test. That night, staff members climbed the towers and guarded the bomb. Alone, Oppenheimer climbed the tower on Sunday afternoon to inspect the bomb and its connections one last time.

A new complication arose Sunday night. A storm brought heavy rains and strong winds that shook the tower. Lightning struck nearby, but did not hit the bomb. Oppenheimer and Groves met with weather forecasters to discuss postponing or canceling the Trinity test. They delayed the test by one and a half hours.

Oppenheimer moved around the area to answer questions and check details. More than a thousand spectators had gathered to watch—army troops, government officials, and the staff from Los Alamos. There was one reporter there—William Lawrence from the *New York Times*. People camped in sleeping bags in tents on a hill called Compagna. Oppenheimer visited the crowds, seeing that they had dinner, passing out suntan lotion, and reviewing safety rules.

Then came the countdown. At about 5:30 A.M., Dr. Joseph L. McKibben of the University of California activated a switch that caused the relayed messages that would set off the bomb. The spectators lay down in protective shelters, with glasses of colored film provided for viewing the explosion. As they waited, they heard music by Tchaikovsky coming from a California radio station that had gotten on their radio frequency.

A few seconds before 5:30 A.M., Monday, July 16, 1945, the bomb exploded. The cloud rose some 12,000 feet above the height of the highest mountain on Earth. After a brief hush came a thunderous roar, which echoed off the surrounding mountains, along with an incredible, multi-colored light. Spectators felt the hot winds with their scorching smell. Instruments at the test site showed that the heat equaled that of the sun, while the light was equal to 20 suns. People in three states saw the brilliant flash.

After the initial silence, the spectators began to celebrate their achievement. George Kistiakowsky, the explosives expert, embraced Robert Oppenheimer, saying, "Oppie, you owe me ten dollars!" He had bet a month's pay against ten dollars that the bomb would work. Oppenheimer supposedly replied, "I haven't got ten dollars with me. I'll pay you later."

The detonation of the world's first nuclear bomb, 5:29 A.M., July 16, 1945.
(Courtesy of Los Alamos National Laboratory)

The test had left a crater in the desert, half a mile in diameter, and the sand had melted. Later, it hardened into a sheet of green glass. The explosion had also killed all the animal life within a radius of one mile. Seeing the powerful results of their work both elated and troubled the scientists. Victor Weisskopf wrote, "All of us, and Oppenheimer more than anyone, were deeply shaken by this event."

The bomb worked. Now military and government officials and scientists debated whether it should be used. Some thought that Japanese commanders should be invited to a demonstration of the bomb, at a site in the Pacific Ocean. Seeing the incredible power of the weapon might persuade them to surrender. Oppenheimer was among those who worried about the outcome if such a test failed. He said that if the bomb was used, it must be aimed at a place that had strong military connections.

President Harry S Truman had taken office after Roosevelt died in April. Once again, he asked Japan for an unconditional surrender, and they refused. Truman decided that only a drastic act would end the war and prevent further casualties. At his order, on August 6, 1945, a B-29 bomber called the *Enola Gay* dropped the Little Boy (uranium) bomb on Hiroshima, Japan. The damage was worse than anything previously seen by humankind: 80,000 people died immediately; 40,000 more were declared "missing." People endured terrible burns and radiation sickness. Two-thirds of Hiroshima lay in ruins.

Japan still did not surrender. Three days after Hiroshima was hit, a Fat Man plutonium bomb was dropped on Nagasaki, destroying 50% of the city. More than 100,000 Japanese were killed and injured. At last, Japan formally ended the war on August 14th.

Oppenheimer received much publicity, with *Time* magazine calling him the "Father of the Atomic Bomb." People marveled at the once-secret government project, which eventually cost $2 billion and produced such fearsome results. The people at Los Alamos were reflective. Their work had helped to end the war, but there was also terrible damage, death, and suffering.

Oppenheimer took a brief vacation with his family. He felt physically and emotionally drained and troubled about the future of atomic weapons. In October, he resigned from his position at Los Alamos, saying that he would once again be a teacher and scientist, not an "armaments manufacturer." At a party and ceremony in his honor, Oppenheimer received a certificate of gratitude from the government. On January 12, 1946, he was awarded the Presidential Medal of Merit. Oppenheimer told journalists, "I'm a little scared of what we built. . . . A scientist cannot hold back progress because he fears what the world will do with his discoveries." On another occasion he said, "Our enemies appeared formidable and the cause in which we were engaged seemed by no means assured of victory."

Oppenheimer's concern about atomic weapons led him to advocate peaceful uses of atomic energy, with a plan for international controls. He wrote government reports about atomic energy and delivered more than 200 public speeches during the next two years. Oppenheimer was frequently asked to explain atomic energy to U.S. legislators at congressional hearings. He expressed

Oppenheimer (wearing his trademark pork pie hat) receives the Army-Navy Award of Excellence from General Leslie R. Groves during a special ceremony at Los Alamos.
(Courtesy of Los Alamos National Laboratory)

the hope that the existence of nuclear weapons would deter future wars.

In 1949, Robert Oppenheimer succeeded Albert Einstein as director of the Institute for Advanced Study in Princeton, New Jersey. Oppenheimer continued as chairperson of the General Advisory Committee of the U.S. Atomic Energy Commission (AEC), a position he had held since 1947. In October, he joined scientists and others who opposed the development of a new and more destructive weapon, the hydrogen bomb.

Many scientists had hoped that the secrecy surrounding atomic energy would end after World War II. But post-war tensions had increased after the Soviet Union assumed control over the governments of several Eastern European countries, isolating them behind what Winston Churchill called an "Iron Curtain." After the

Soviet Union tested its own atomic weapons in summer 1949, Americans feared what they would do with them. Some towns and individuals built bomb shelters as anti-Soviet feeling spread throughout the nation.

This picture from the Institute for Advanced Study shows Oppenheimer in his office while serving as director there.
(Courtesy of the Institute for Advanced Study, Princeton; photo by Alan Richards)

In 1951, the Atomic Energy Commission announced that the H-bomb, or superbomb, would indeed be funded and built. Oppenheimer feared that most Americans did not know the hazards and damage that H-bombs could cause. He believed that voters should get accurate information about these issues. Because Oppenheimer was still involved in plans to develop atomic power plants—secret information at the time—he had to pass another security check, and was again "cleared" to continue working with the AEC.

During the early 1950s, called the cold war years, fear and animosity toward Communist Russia swelled in America. Senator Joseph McCarthy led investigations into the loyalty of various citizens, especially those in public life. People were asked to swear and/or sign loyalty oaths to the United States. Often their past and present political associations were examined.

In 1953 Robert Oppenheimer was investigated by a government committee. He was told that a military security report contained information about him that was "unfavorable," and that he was accused of having associated with Communists during the 1930s. It did not help that he had been vocally opposing the development of the hydrogen bomb.

At the April 1954 hearing, numerous people, including General Leslie Groves, and the Federation of American Scientists defended Oppenheimer, protesting against his trial and other such investigations. The FBI reported that investigators had not seen Oppenheimer do anything suspicious during the war. After a four-week hearing, Oppenheimer was cleared of the charge of treason. But the committee voted 4–1 that he was a security risk. It advised that Oppenheimer be denied access to military secrets, so the Atomic Energy Commission canceled Oppenheimer's contract. Like Linus Pauling and others, Oppenheimer was a troubling reminder that some Americans had been persecuted for expressing opinions about moral issues that arose from scientific discoveries.

The hearing and its aftermath deeply upset Oppenheimer and his family. He continued teaching and spent more time with his children. The Institute for Advanced Study reappointed him as director in 1954. He also lectured in America and other countries. In 1956, in Chicago, he said, "In a free world, if it is to remain free, we must maintain . . . the opportunity for a man to learn anything. We need to do more: we need to cherish man's curiosity, his understanding, his love, so that he may indeed learn what is new and hard and deep."

In a speech called "Tree of Knowledge," which he gave at the University of Wisconsin in 1959, Oppenheimer encouraged people to improve their communities and the larger world, or as he called it, "the human community." He said, "[This] will help to see us through one of the most peculiar episodes in man's history."

As McCarthyism faded, more people agreed that the case against Oppenheimer had been unjust. Prominent people urged the Atomic Energy Commission to give Oppenheimer the Fermi Award. In December 1963, President Lyndon Johnson presented this honor to Oppenheimer, saying, "Your leadership in the development of an outstanding school of theoretical physics in the United States and your contributions to our basic knowledge make your achievements unique in the scientific world." Observers reported that Oppenheimer was visibly moved. He said, "I think it is just possible, Mr. President, that it has taken some charity and courage for you to make this award today. That would seem to be a good augury for all our futures."

Oppenheimer spent his last years writing and lecturing about the philosophy of science and the way that science affects society. In 1966, he retired from the Institute for Advanced Study, having been diagnosed with cancer of the throat. He died in Princeton on February 18, 1967, at age 62. Hundreds of colleagues, friends, and officials attended his memorial service at Princeton University. They praised Oppenheimer as teacher, scientist, and citizen.

He had trained a generation of American physicists who went on to teach others and make important discoveries. "He transmitted to his students a feeling of the beauty of the logical structure of physics and an excitement in the development of the science," claimed Isidor I. Rabi, a former student. Of Oppenheimer's unique success as director at Los Alamos, Enrico Fermi said, "He was very close to indispensable. You think someone else might have come along—but you never know."

The former child prodigy and master of both arts and sciences had brought the world squarely into the atomic age. Robert Oppenheimer helped to end a devastating war, and he led his nation to a scientific victory during one of the most turbulent periods in human history.

Chronology

April 22, 1904	Robert Oppenheimer born in New York City
1921	graduates from School for Ethical Culture
1925	receives B.S. in physics from Harvard University
1926–27	begins graduate studies at Cambridge and University of Göttingen
1927	receives Ph.D. in physics from the University of Göttingen
1928–29	continues post-graduate studies abroad at University of Leyden and Technical Institute in Switzerland
1929	appointed to physics departments at both the University of California at Berkeley and Caltech at Pasadena
1942	agrees to become coordinator of atomic research at the Office of Scientific Research and Development, the government project aiming to build atomic weapons; his specific unit became known as the Manhattan District Project at Los Alamos
July 16, 1945	supervises the first atomic bomb test at the Trinity site, near Alamogordo, New Mexico
1945	Atomic bombs dropped on Japan (Hiroshima, August 6; and Nagasaki, August 9); Japan surrenders on August 14

1945	Oppenheimer leaves Los Alamos in October; goes back to teach at Caltech
1947	appointed director of the Institute for Advanced Study in Princeton, New Jersey; chairperson General Advisory Committee of the U.S. Atomic Energy Commission (AEC)
1953	Atomic Energy Commission suspends his security clearance pending a hearing and review of his past political activities and associations
1954	is barred from government work in physics after hearing results in a vote not to restore his security clearance
1963	receives the AEC's Enrico Fermi Award on December 2 for outstanding contributions to science of physics
February 18, 1967	dies in Princeton, New Jersey, at age 62

Further Reading

Bethe, H. A. "Oppenheimer: Where He Was There Was Always Life and Excitement." *Science*, Vol. 155 (March 3, 1967): 1080–84. A memoir of Oppenheimer written by a famous physicist who worked on the Manhattan Project at Los Alamos

Goueff, Stephane. *Manhattan Project*. Boston: Little, Brown, 1967. A history of the building of the atomic bomb and the military and scientific work involved in the project.

Groves, Leslie R. *Now It Can Be Told*. New York: Harper, 1962. Memoir of the Manhattan Project by its military director.

Laurence, William L. *Dawn Over Zero: The Story of the Atomic Bomb*. New York: Knopf, 1947. A prominent science writer (and the only journalist to see the Trinity test) describes the Manhattan Project.

Oppenheimer, J. Robert. "The Age of Science: 1900–1950." *Scientific American*, Vol. 183, No. 3 (September 1950): 20–23. Oppenheimer analyzes scientific achievements during the first half of the 20th century.

———. *The Open Mind*. New York: Simon and Schuster, 1955. Contains the physicist's philosophical views.

———. *Science and the Common Understanding* New York: Simon and Schuster, 1954. Addresses the relationship between modern science and society.

Rabi, I. I. et al. *Oppenheimer: The Story of One of the Most Remarkable Personalities of Our Time*. New York: Scribner's, 1969. A view of Oppenheimer's life and work by a former student and others who worked on the Manhattan Project.

Shepley, James R. and Clay Blair Jr. *The Hydrogen Bomb*. New York: David McKay, 1954. History of the more destructive weapons developed after the first atomic bombs.

Smith, Alice Kimball and Charles Weiner, eds. *Robert Oppenheimer: Letters and Recollections*. Cambridge, Mass.: Harvard, 1980. Contains personal and professional letters Oppenheimer wrote during teaching career and Manhattan Project.

James Dewey Watson:
Pioneer of Molecular Biology

James Watson in the laboratory.
(Courtesy of the National Library of Medicine)

A remarkable article appeared in the April 25, 1953, issue of *Nature*, a British scientific journal. It began with these words: "We wish to suggest a structure for the salt of deoxyribonucleic acid (DNA). This structure has novel features which are of considerable biological interest." The authors of this paper knew that there was tremendous interest in DNA, the material that makes up chromosomes found inside all cells. The DNA molecule holds and transmits vital information about heredity and other life processes. Scientists all over the world had long been eager to understand how DNA was constructed and how it worked.

Announcing this landmark discovery were a British physicist, Francis H. C. Crick, and an American biologist, James Dewey Watson. They had worked together in Cambridge, England, for nearly two years to figure out the structure of DNA. They hoped that their research would provide important clues about how DNA transmits what has been called the "code of life."

Watson and Crick put together a three-dimensional model of DNA. They went on to produce a theory about the way in which the molecule operates to pass on hereditary traits. Scientists hearing about the Watson and Crick model were excited. In the past, research had focused on organisms, then on the smaller units, or cells, that make up an organism's tissues. Now science focused on even smaller units—the molecules within the cells. Work on the DNA molecule thus developed with a still new field in science: molecular biology. Molecular biologists study chemical structures and life processes at the molecular level. A molecule is the smallest part of a substance that retains that substance's properties. In the case of DNA, for example, the molecule is the smallest part of the substance that contains all the traits of DNA. Molecular biologists also study the working of proteins, other nucleic acids inside cells, and enzymes (proteins that speed up chemical reactions in cells).

Many people regard the discovery of the structure of DNA as the foremost biological achievement of the 20th century. It is certainly at least among the most important discoveries. Since Watson and Crick revealed their model, scientists from several fields of science—genetics, biophysics, and biochemistry—have worked to map the locations of genes on various chromosomes, trying to "crack the DNA code." As a result of such research, scientists have been able to create DNA in the laboratory. Another controversial offshoot of DNA research is genetic engineering, the actual changing of genes through such techniques as cutting and splicing.

James Dewey Watson was born in Chicago, Illinois, on April 6, 1928. Watson attended public schools while growing up in Chicago. Like many famous scientists, as a child James Watson showed that he was highly intelligent. Watson was among the young people who appeared as contestants on a famous radio program called the "Quiz Kids." Children from various parts of America showed their academic ability as they took turns answering questions during the program.

Watson grew up during the era of the Great Depression of the 1930s and the eventful 1940s, which included World War II. During this time the family experienced financial difficulties. Watson's mother worked in the admissions office at the University of Chicago. Watson lived at home and commuted by streetcar when he entered this university at the young age of fifteen. During the previous winter, Enrico Fermi and his team had achieved the first nuclear chain reaction in a lab set up at the University of Chicago squash courts. But James Watson would not have heard about this secret event at the time.

Watson earned a B.S. in zoology in 1947. He enjoyed watching and studying birds and thought he might become a bird curator, perhaps at the American Museum of Natural History in New York City. Following graduation from college he spent the summer at the University of Michigan, studying ornithology, the science of birds. Although he would later become one of the most celebrated scientists of his time, Watson claims that as an undergraduate student he avoided "chemistry or physics courses which looked of even moderate difficulty."

During his senior year, though, Watson had developed an interest in genes. Lacking a strong chemistry background, he said that "it was my hope that the gene might be solved without my learning any chemistry."

Watson eventually did spend time in a chemistry laboratory after he entered graduate school in zoology at the University of Indiana. His professors advised him to study organic chemistry (the chemistry of living things). By that time, Watson recalls, he had a "serious desire to learn genetics." He had been impressed by Erwin Schrödinger's book *What Is Life?*, published in 1944. In it, Schrödinger discusses the possible atomic and molecular bases of life. A physicist, Schrödinger used the newly developing theories of quantum mechanics to consider the nature of the gene.

There were some outstanding geneticists at the University of Indiana, including Hermann Joseph Muller, who had worked with Thomas Hunt Morgan at Columbia University. Muller became famous in his own right when he used X rays on *Drosophila* (fruit fly) chromosomes to cause controlled mutations (changes in the traits passed on to new generations). By 1936, he was known as the scientist who had altered forms of life in a lab.

Watson received his Ph.D. in 1950. He wrote his doctoral thesis about the lethal effect of X rays on bacterial viruses (viruses that attack bacteria). His graduate supervisor, Salvador Luria, was known for his extensive studies of these viruses, called bacteriophages, or phages for short. Phages are the simplest forms of all viruses. (Viruses are minute acellular parasites.) The scientists who were studying phages began wondering if viruses were essentially naked genes, made entirely of DNA.

The next year, Watson received a grant from the National Research Council to study bacteriophages at the University of Copenhagen, Denmark. In Europe, he heard enthusiastic discussions about the new frontiers to be explored in genetics, such as learning the structure of the DNA molecule. Scientists expected to discover how DNA transmitted hereditary information once they understood how it was constructed. Watson recalls that these talks inspired his desire "to learn more about the structure of the molecules which the geneticists talked about so passionately."

In spring 1951, Watson attended a scientific conference in Naples, Italy. There he met Maurice Wilkins, a New Zealand–born biophysicist who was studying DNA with Dr. Rosalind Franklin and others at King's College in London. They had taken X-ray diffraction pictures of crystallized DNA—that is, they had passed X rays through samples of DNA that had been made into crystals, directing the rays onto photographic film. Then they examined the patterns on the developed photographs. These patterns could be used to interpret the DNA structure—the types and positions of atoms in the molecule. X-ray crystallography, as this process was called, had been used by American Linus Pauling and other scientists to gather clues about the arrangement of atoms in various molecules.

Seeing these X-ray diffraction photos of DNA, Watson says, "A potential key to the secret of life was impossible to push out of my mind." He decided to study DNA at Cavendish Laboratory, a famous scientific research center at Cambridge University in Cambridge, England. But the National Research Council would not keep funding Watson if he studied DNA instead of bacteriophages, so Watson got a new grant from the National Foundation for Infantile Paralysis.

At Cambridge, Watson met Francis Harry Compton Crick, who had been born in 1916, in Northampton, England. After being trained as a physicist, he helped to develop radar devices and underwater explosives used by the British Admiralty during World War II. After the war, Crick conducted research at Cavendish Laboratory. He became fascinated with the biological research being done at that time and read extensively about molecules, finally concentrating on the DNA molecule. When Watson met Crick at Cavendish, they realized that they shared a strong interest in DNA.

Other scientists were studying DNA. Some people had begun calling these efforts the "race for the DNA molecule." Maurice Wilkins and Rosalind Franklin were working on DNA at King's College in London. In California, Linus Pauling had studied DNA from time to time. He was known for his remarkable work on the structure of proteins during the 1940s and 1950s. Watson found out that Pauling wanted to see copies of the DNA X-ray pictures taken by Rosalind Franklin and Maurice Wilkins. These pictures hinted that the DNA molecule took the form of a helix—a shape that resembles a spiral. It seemed to be the same width all along its length. Knowing that DNA might have a helical shape was a great help to scientists, but many questions still remained. For example, how many strands of atoms did the helix contain? And what kinds of atoms made up the inside and the outside of the helix.

As was true in the development of atomic energy, the eventual discovery of DNA's structure and function built upon the work of many scientists working in different places over a period of years. DNA was first isolated and examined in 1869 by a Swiss chemist, Johann Friedrich Miescher. Miescher had extracted a pasty gray powder from human white blood cells. Because this substance came from the cell nucleus, he named it nuclein. (Later, this substance was found to be an acid and was renamed nucleic acid.) Miescher had discovered DNA. However, at the time, scientists did not understand that it plays a vital role in heredity and growth.

Other discoveries followed as Gregor Mendel, Hugo de Vries, Thomas Hunt Morgan, and Herman Muller, among others, studied patterns of inheritance in living things. They found that hereditary traits are located and linked on genes, which are located on chromosomes, almost always found inside the cell nucleus. Still, no one knew how these chromosomes could hold so much detailed information. How could such a wide variety of traits be encoded? How did DNA reproduce itself, causing like to produce like, in so many different kinds of living things?

In 1925, Pheobus A. Levene added some chemical information about DNA. Levene found that the DNA molecule is a series of nucleotides, each of which holds three molecules within the larger DNA molecule. The nucleotides consist of a five-sided sugar molecule, a phosphate molecule (containing hydrogen, oxygen, and phosphorus), and a base molecule that is able to bond with (join with) hydrogen. This verified one of Miescher's findings, that DNA holds phosphorus. Still, nobody knew the total number of nucleotides that DNA contained or the way in which they were organized.

Also during the 1920s, scientists realized that there was more than one kind of nucleic acid. The other nucleic acid became known as RNA—short for ribonucleic acid. What role did RNA play in growth and heredity? scientists now wondered.

Information accumulated during the 1930s and 1940s. It seemed that DNA was a rather large molecule and took the form of a long, repeating, threadlike chain. Studies by Americans George W. Beadle and Edward L. Tatum indicated that DNA regulates growth. These researchers found that DNA controls the production of enzymes.

In 1944 Oswald Avery and other scientists at Rockefeller Institute in New York City concluded that DNA could transform one kind of bacteria into another type. They transplanted DNA from one strain of bacterium to another. The transplanted DNA changed the appearance of the second bacterium.

Later, in 1952, Alfred Hershey and Martha Chase used radioactively labeled DNA to show that it was the DNA from a bacteriophage, not the protein, that entered cells. Here was evidence that DNA is the information carrier in the cell nucleus.

During the late 1940s, Austrian-American scientist Erwin Chargaff studied cells from many different organisms. He found DNA in the nuclei of all the cells he studied. Chargaff also learned important things about the chemical bases—adenine (A), guanine (G), thymine (T), and cytosine (C)—found in DNA. He calculated that the amount of guanine in DNA was about the same as the amount of cytosine. The same relationship held true for adenine and thymine. And Chargaff's work showed that DNA contained the same chemicals even when taken from very different organisms, such as a fish, mouse, or fly. More and more, DNA research looked like the key to answer questions about the processes of life and growth.

Information about the DNA structure was enhanced by the X-ray crystallography photographs of DNA molecules. Pictures by Wilkins, Franklin, and others showed that DNA molecules taken from a variety of living things had the same outline on the photos: a helix. Wilkins commented, "The basic molecular configuration has great simplicity." As with the chemical studies, there was nothing in these pictures to explain how very different traits (such as those found in fish versus humans) could be transmitted by a molecule with a similar shape and chemical make-up. Scientists were more curious than ever to solve this puzzle.

With this information and much interest, Watson tackled DNA at Cavendish. He and Crick used X-ray diffraction photographs to estimate the distances among the various atoms in the DNA molecule, making written calculations. Watson recalls that they used "common sense," along with knowledge about "which atoms like to sit together." Some of Watson's knowledge about the latter subject had come from reading Linus Pauling's book about chemical bonds.

Watson also knew about Pauling's successful model-making methods. He and Crick used metal, wires, and other materials to construct possible models of the molecule. Before them were the various parts—pieces to represent the DNA bases, the five-sided sugar molecules, and the phosphates—but they did not fit together properly in any of the combinations the two scientists tried.

Watson and Crick worked 18 months before the eventual structure took shape. They constructed a coil that made one complete turn after every 10 phosphate groups, as they knew it should. They alternated the sugars with the phosphates, forming the backbone or frame of the molecule. After many calculations and model-building sessions, they came up with the idea of a double, instead of a single, helix. The double helix was two spirals, intertwined, climbing upward. The sugar-phosphate chains formed the intertwining spirals of the molecule.

Finding where to place the bases—adenine, thymine, guanine, and cytosine—was difficult. Each had a different shape. The two larger ones, A and G, belonged to a chemical group called purines; the two smaller ones, C and T, belonged to the group called pyramidines. Watson and Crick could not determine how far from each other these bases should be. Nor did they know exactly how the bases related to each other.

As they continued to study the framework of the molecule and to think about the chemical principles involved, it seemed that the bases should be located inside the helices. There was room for two bases to fit between sugar molecules that were opposite each other. Yet two purines were too large to fit inside the strands of the helix; the two pyrimidines were too small.

The research by Chargaff had indicated the proportions of the four bases inside the molecule. This suggested that a purine and pyramidine base might be paired. Furthermore, it indicated that adenine (a longer base) might join with thymine (a shorter base), while guanine (a longer base) and cytosine (a shorter base) paired up as well. If that were so, the two strands of the helix would be complementary, or parallel. If one strand contained the bases C-A-G-T-A-A-C, the opposite strand would have these: G-T-C-A-T-T-G. Furthermore, joining shorter bases with longer ones would result in "steps" going across the spiralling staircase—steps that were equal in size.

Those final days of calculations and model-making were busy ones. Watson later wrote, "It seemed almost unbelievable that the DNA structure was solved, that the answer was incredibly exciting, and that our names would be associated with the double helix as Pauling's was with the alpha helix [an earlier discovery]."

The metal parts for their models had been made to order in a workshop. As Watson and Crick arrived at their final designs, they needed new parts in order to test their ideas. Within the next few hours, the workshop had soldered the new materials together. Watson described what followed: "The brightly shining metal plates were then immediately used to make a model in which for the first time all the DNA components were present. In about an hour I had arranged the atoms in positions which satisfied both the X-ray data and the laws of stereochemistry [a branch of chemistry that deals with the spatial arrangement of atoms or groups of atoms that compose a molecule]. The resulting helix was right-handed with the two chains running in opposite directions. Only one person can easily play with a model, and so Francis did not try to check my work until I backed away and said that I thought everything fitted."

The model looked like a long twisted ladder with a frame made of sugar and phosphate molecules. The steps of the ladder were the four bases (A, G, C, and T), attached to the sides at right angles. Here was the DNA molecule at last: a tiny part of a chromosome, yet containing within itself hundreds of genes.

But the work was not yet finished. Watson and Crick spent several days checking the measurements of their DNA model with

Watson and Crick examine the DNA model they built in 1953 at Cavendish Laboratory.
(Courtesy of Cold Spring Harbor Laboratory)

a measuring stick. They made sure that the atoms in each nucleotide were placed correctly in regard to each other. They asked William H. Bragg, a prominent British physicist, to examine the model. As Watson remembers, Bragg was sick but was excited "when he heard that Crick and I had thought up an ingenious DNA structure which might be important to biology." He agreed that the model embodied every fact that was then known about DNA.

The next step was to announce their thrilling discovery. The article they wrote for *Nature* was ready on the the last weekend in

March 1953. Watson's sister Elizabeth was then visiting him so they asked her to type the article. "We told her that she was participating in perhaps the most famous event in biology since Darwin's book," wrote Watson. "Francis and I stood over her as she typed the nine-hundred-word article. . . ."

On April 2, 1953, the article was sent to *Nature*. After describing their molecular model, Watson and Crick wrote that the double helix they had proposed "immediately suggests a possible copying mechanism for the genetic material." In other words, the structure suggested the method by which DNA duplicates itself. It appeared that the DNA helix unwinds and the two sides of the helix split apart. The chemicals needed to build more DNA molecules are present inside the cell nucleus. These units attach themselves to the opened-up DNA chain, resulting in two new molecules.

Watson had been somewhat reluctant to discuss the genetic significance of the model. What if they were wrong? But Crick's opinion prevailed.

Not everyone accepted the DNA model or the theories Watson and Crick, along with Maurice Wilkins, had proposed. Yet evidence from X rays and other laboratory tests continued to support both the Watson-Crick model and their ideas about duplication. Five weeks after their electrifying announcement, Watson and Crick published another article in *Nature*, discussing the "genetic implications of the structure."

After Watson completed this work, he left the Cavendish Laboratories. Crick continued to study DNA. He concluded that the order of the bases (the steps across the DNA "staircase") is what determines the DNA code. The number, order, and types of chemical units in the DNA molecule are responsible for an organism's genetic make-up. So many kinds of traits are possible because millions of combinations and arrangements of the four bases (A, C, T, and G) along the DNA strands are possible. This would explain the incredible diversity found in living things. As Crick explained, "Such an arrangement can carry an enormous amount of information."

Further studies showed that DNA regulates other body activities for health and growth. It is the DNA molecule that tells cells how long to keep growing. In some cases, it directs the regrowth of tissues that have been damaged.

In fall 1953, James Watson became a Senior Research Fellow at the California Institute of Technology (Caltech). Using the techniques of X-ray crystallography, he studied RNA. Studying

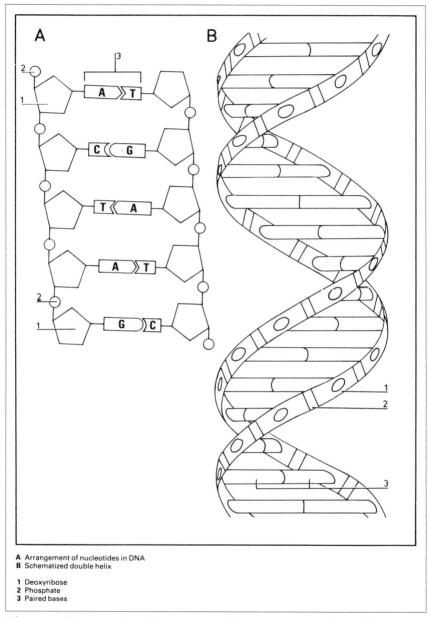

A Arrangement of nucleotides in DNA
B Schematized double helix

1 Deoxyribose
2 Phosphate
3 Paired bases

These two diagrams show the structure of DNA. Diagram A shows the arrangement of nucleotides in DNA. Diagram B is a schematic double helix. In both diagrams, 1 is deoxyribose, 2 is phosphate, and 3 is the paired bases.
(Copyright DIAGRAM)

RNA, different scientists found that it worked with DNA to manufacture proteins in cells.

In 1955, Watson again worked with Francis Crick at Cambridge to study the structures of viruses. They completed this work and published their findings a year later. Watson returned to the United States to join the biology department at Harvard University in Cambridge, Massachusetts. In the following years, the laboratory Watson set up at Harvard would train some accomplished molecular biologists.

With Crick and Wilkins, James Watson accepted the 1962 Nobel Prize for physiology or medicine. The three shared the honor and $50,000 prize money for discovering the structure of DNA. (Some historians believe that if Rosalind Franklin had not died in 1958, she might also have been included.) As he accepted his prize, the 34-year-old Watson called this "the second greatest moment of my life." Later in the speech, he commented that "good science as a way of life is difficult. . . . We must thus believe strongly in our ideas, often to the point where they may seem tiresome and bothersome and even arrogant to our colleagues. . . ."

After leaving Sweden, where they had received the Nobel Prize, Watson and James Kendrew, co-recipient of the Nobel Prize for chemistry that year, visited CERN (the international nuclear physics research center) in Geneva, Switzerland. They met with physicist Leo Szilard, who had become a molecular biologist. Szilard recommended that another international lab like CERN be founded, to promote biological research. Watson and other scientists supported this goal, and as a result of their efforts in the following years, EMBO—the European Molecular Biology Organization—became official in May 1979, with Kendrew as director. EMBO is located in Heidelberg, Germany, with outstations in Hamburg, Germany, and in Grenoble, France. It awards research fellowships to talented scientists from many countries.

Returning to Harvard, Watson continued to teach and began writing a personal account of the discovery of the DNA molecule, *The Double Helix*, published in 1968. That same year, Watson became director of Cold Spring Harbor Laboratory, a biological station on the North Shore of Long Island, New York. There, he has developed a post-graduate program in DNA science and has guided important studies of tumor virology, adding to knowledge about cancer genes and the molecular basis of cancer. The laboratory is known throughout the world for its research on cell biochemistry. About 4,000 visiting scientists from various countries attend meetings and courses at Cold Spring Harbor every year.

During the 1970s, author Horace Judson interviewed Watson about his work. Speaking about the labs and teaching programs at Cold Spring Harbor, Watson said he would "like it to be a place where advanced science can be done, and also where people can come to talk about it occasionally, talk about it in a formal atmosphere of meetings and advanced courses—and sometimes to make it more permanent by putting it into books."

Watson in a recent photo.
(Courtesy of the National Center for Human Genome Research,
National Institutes of Health)

James D. Watson has continued working in the fields of bacterial genetics and DNA research. In 1981, he published (with John Tooze) *The DNA Story: A Documentary History of Gene Cloning*. In all, he has published dozens of scientific articles and five books. He and his wife, the former Elizabeth Lewis, have two sons, Rufus and Duncan.

During the 1970s and 1980s, studies of DNA led to many practical, and controversial, results. Scientists found that certain enzymes will cut and recombine segments of DNA in the chromosomes of various bacteria. The result has been another growing branch of molecular biology—recombinant DNA technology. DNA from different bacteria have been mixed together to make another—recombinant—DNA. DNA has also been produced in test tubes. In 1982, human insulin was made by the use of recombinant DNA methods. In 1983 at the University of Pennsylvania human DNA was transplanted into mice. A working human gene that produces a growth hormone in humans produced "supermouse," a mouse twice normal size.

Scientists have found better ways to analyze the DNA in chromosomes. They can diagnose sickle-cell anemia, among other hereditary diseases, before birth. They have developed methods of analyzing the sequence of DNA on chromosomes, with the goal of locating all the human genes. This idea of finding a complete genetic "blueprint" developed into a program called the Human Genome Initiative, administered by the National Institutes of Health. James D. Watson became an associate director of that program in 1988 and from 1989 to 1992 was the director, while still serving as director of Cold Spring Harbor Laboratory. Because the Human Genome project is so complex (there may be 3 billion base pairs to analyze on human chromosomes), Watson suggested in May 1989 that nations throughout the world work together on the project.

The genome project is one of many outgrowths of the discovery of the double helix in 1953—a finding that ranks with the harnessing of atomic energy as one of the most momentous scientific events of the 20th century. The research and insights of James Dewey Watson have both sparked and sustained this explosion of knowledge and research.

Chronology

▬▬▬▬▬

April 6, 1928	James Dewey Watson born in Chicago, Illinois
1947	receives B.S. in zoology, University of Chicago
1950	receives Ph.D. in zoology, University of Indiana
1950–51	conducts research with H. M. Kalckar at University of Copenhagen
1951	begins research at Cavendish Laboratory, Cambridge University in England
1953	determines, together with Francis Crick, the molecular model for the DNA molecule
1953–55	appointed senior research fellow in biology, Caltech
1955–56	conducts research at Cavendish Laboratory
1956–58	appointed assistant professor of biology, Harvard University
1958–61	appointed associate professor of biology, Harvard University
1960	receives the Albert Lasker Prize, awarded by the American Public Health Association
1961–76	appointed professor of biology, Harvard University
1962	awarded the Nobel Prize in medicine (with Crick and Wilkins)
1965	publishes *Molecular Biology of the Gene*

1968–	appointed director of the Cold Spring Harbor Laboratory
1968	publishes *The Double Helix*
1971	awarded the John J. Carty Gold Medal of the National Academy of Sciences
1977	receives Presidential Medal of Freedom
1981	becomes honorary fellow of the Royal Society of London; publishes *The DNA Story*, written with John Tooze
1983	publishes *Molecular Biology of the Cell*, with Bruce Alberts, Dennis Bray, Julian Lewis, Martin Ruff, and Keith Roberts; and *Recombinant DNA: A Short Course*, with John Tooze and Davit T. Kurtz.
1988–89	serves as associate director for the National Institutes of Health for the Human Genome Initiative
1989–92	serves as director of National Center for Human Genome Research of the National Institutes of Health

Further Reading

Dickson, David. "Watson Floats Up a Plan to Carve Up the Genome." *Science*, Vol. 244 (May 5, 1989): 621–622. Watson discusses the human genome project.

Golob, Richard, and Eric Brus. *The Almanac of Science and Technology: What's New and What's Known.* New York: Harcourt, 1990. Summarizes the development of molecular biology, DNA research, and recent advances in genetic engineering.

Gore, Rick, et al. "The New Biology." *National Geographic*, Vol. 150, No. 3 (September 1976), 355–399. Explains the structure and functions of the cell, and its DNA; striking color illustrations and photographs.

Judson, Horace. *The Eighth Day of Creation*. New York: Simon and Schuster, 1979. A comprehensive account of the development of genetics and molecular biology, including DNA research, with extensive footnotes. For more advanced students.

Seidler, Ned and Rick Gore. "Seven Giants Who Led the Way." *National Geographic*, Vol. 150, No. 3 (September 1976), 401–407. Overview of landmark discoveries in biology, made by Leeuwenhoek, Darwin, Mendel, Pasteur, Morgan, and Watson and Crick.

Watson, James Dewey. *The Double Helix*. New York: Atheneum, 1968. Watson's personal account of the research leading up to the discovery of the structure of the DNA molecule.

Watson, James Dewey (with John Tooze). *The DNA Story: A Documentary of Gene Cloning*. San Francisco: W.H. Freeman, 1981. Detailed account of recent research and uses of gene cloning; includes numerous documents and letters from scientists involved in the field.

Weaver, Robert F. "Changing Life's Genetic Blueprint." *National Geographic*, Vol. 166, No. 6 (December 1984), 818–833. Written by a molecular biologist, the article describes the amazing work being done in biotechnology.

Williams, Trevor I. *Science: A History of Discovery in the Twentieth Century*. Oxford: Oxford University Press, 1990. Recounts the major scientific discoveries of the 20th century; numerous photographs, charts, and diagrams. Time lines place events in their historical context, and text describes the impact of scientific events on society; appendix with brief biographies of leading scientists.

Index

Numbers in **boldface** indicate main headings.

Index

Index

Index

Index